Virginia Woolf's Quarrel with Grieving

Virginia Woolf's Quarrel with Grieving

Mark Spilka

University of Nebraska Press
Lincoln and London

Excerpts from the following books by Virginia Woolf are reprinted by permission of the Author's Literary Estate, the Hogarth Press, and Harcourt Brace Jovanovich, Inc.: *Mrs. Dalloway; To the Lighthouse; Moments of Being*, edited by Jeanne Schulkind; and *A Writer's Diary*, edited by Leonard Woolf; copyright 1925, 1927 by Harcourt Brace Jovanovich, Inc.; copyright 1953, 1955 by Leonard Woolf; copyright 1976 by Quentin Bell and Angelica Garnett; copyright 1953, 1954 by Leonard Woolf.

Library of Congress Cataloging in Publication Data

Spilka, Mark.
    Virginia Woolf's quarrel with grieving.

    Bibliography: p. 135
    Includes index.
    1. Woolf, Virginia Stephen, 1882–1941—Criticism and interpretation.
2. Death in literature.   3. Grief in literature.   I. Title.
PR6045.Q72Z8775   823'.912   80–11792
ISBN 0–8032–4120–8

for that gallant survivor
Ruth Ann Dane Farnum Spilka

Contents

Acknowledgments

As readers familiar with my essay "Parties and Funerals: An Academic Confession" *(College English* 35 [January 1974]: 367–80) will understand, my thinking on this subject began during my tenure as chairman of the Brown English Department (1968–73) when an unusual series of deaths forced us often to act in lieu of family and to devise new ways to mourn lost friends and colleagues. So my first acknowledgment is to the memory of Richard Patrick, Andrew Turnbull, Hallie Bradner, Joan Scholes, Charles Philbrick, S. Foster Damon, and Rosalie Colie—and long before them, the father whom I have since learned how to mourn, Harvey Spilka.

My debts to the living are fortunately more numerous. I owe thanks to David Lodge of the University of Birmingham in England and to Thomas Blues of the University of Kentucky at Lexington for the chance to test against their students an early version of chapter 2. I owe thanks also to the editors of several journals for the chance to air and improve the following modified versions of chapters 2, 4, and 5 in their pages, and for permission to reincorporate and expand upon them here: "The Robber in the

Bedroom; or, The Thief of Love: A Woolfian Grieving in Six Novels and Two Memoirs" (*Critical Inquiry* 5 [Summer 1979]: 663–82); "On Mrs. Dalloway's Absent Grief: A Psycho-Literary Speculation" (*Contemporary Literature* 20 [Summer 1979]: 318–38); and "On Lily Briscoe's Absent Grief: A Psycho-Literary Speculation" (*Criticism* 21 [Winter 1979]: 1–33). A few passages from chapters 1 and 6 have also appeared in "New Life in the Works: Some Recent Woolf Studies" (*Novel: A Forum on Fiction* 12 [Winter 1979]: 169–84).

I want to thank also the National Endowment for the Humanities for the chance to pursue my larger project, "New Literary Quarrels with Tenderness," to which the present study is related. I am indebted also to Professors George Ford, Julian Moynahan, and Patricia Spacks for their support of my NEH project; to my honors student Bettye Ann Blatman for the gift copy of *Moments of Being* which got me going on Woolf; to my graduate student Linda White Stormes for problem-solving opportunities in pursuit of her master's thesis on religious yearning in the novels of Virginia Woolf; to Ruth Oppenheim and her cohorts Lorraine Basile, Shirley Rodrigues, and Marilyn Tobin of the Brown English Department for innumerable mailings and assistances; to the librarians at Brown and Cambridge University for scholarly services; to nameless professional readers whose reactions, whether sympathetic or obtuse, sometimes actually helped me to improve my manuscript; to Becky Mizer, whose typing really did improve it; and most of all, to that extraordinarily empathetic and insightful person, Ruth Spilka, whose training as a psychiatric social worker served me in good stead, when in our chill Cambridge rooms she helped me to thresh out the warmer premises by which this study began, and on which it still proceeds.

Virginia Woolf's Quarrel with Grieving

Abbreviations

CE   *Collected Essays.* Edited by Leonard Woolf. 2 vols. London: Chatto and Windus, 1966, 1967.

DVW   *The Diary of Virginia Woolf.* Edited by Anne Olivier Bell. Vol. 1: 1915–19. Vol. 2: 1920–24. London: Hogarth Press, 1977, 1978.

LVW   *The Letters of Virginia Woolf.* Edited by Nigel Nicolson and Joanne Trautmann. Vol. 1: 1888–1912. Vol. 2: 1919–22. New York and London: Harvest, 1977.

MB   *Moments of Being: Unpublished Autobiographical Writings.* Edited by Jeanne Schulkind. New York and London: Harcourt Brace Jovanovich, 1976.

MD   *Mrs. Dalloway.* New York: Harbrace, 1925.

MDP   *Mrs. Dalloway's Party: A Short Story Sequence.* Edited by Stella McNichol. London: Hogarth Press, 1973.

QB   Quentin Bell. *Virginia Woolf: A Biography.* 2 vols. New York: Harvest, 1972.

TP   *The Pargiters: The Novel-Essay Portion of "The Years."* Edited by Mitchell A. Leaska. New York: New York Public Library and Readex Books, 1977.

TTL   *To the Lighthouse.* New York: Harbrace, 1927.

TW   *The Waves.* New York: Harcourt Brace, 1931.

TY   *The Years.* Frogmore, St. Albans, Herts.: Triad/Panther, 1977.

VO   *The Voyage Out.* Harmondsworth, Middlesex: Penguin, 1975.

WD   *A Writer's Diary.* Edited by Leonard Woolf. London: Hogarth Press, 1975.

1 Converging Views

Behold then, the blue madonna streaked with tears. This is my funeral service. We have no ceremonies, only private dirges and no conclusions, only violent sensations, each separate. Nothing that has been said meets our case.

Bernard in *The Waves*

In *Truth to Life*, a book on nineteenth-century biography, A. O. J. Cockshut remarks on certain lines of continuity between the modern Bloomsbury writers, E. M. Forster and Virginia Woolf, and their Clapham forebears of the early nineteenth century: their common cliquishness as members of exclusive, self-sufficient sets; their concern with salvation through proper beliefs, attitudes, habits; their "determined, solid, serious unconventionality." Even their lines of difference express such continuity, as with their opposing attitudes toward sex and death. Thus:

> In his life of his great-aunt Marianne Thornton, daughter of a leading Clapham figure, [Forster] writes with sharp distaste of an emotional death scene of 1814, and of the subsequent literary embroidery of grief: 'He was ill. He died. His family and his friends were with him. Why cannot his daughter leave it at that . . . ?'
>
> We remember that in Forster's own novels the characters often die in relative clauses. The prudery of our century about death would have seemed as strange to the Victorians as their own

1

variety does now. But the principle on which reticence is based seems to be identical; sex (or death) is held to be so important that one must never speak of it. And this startling paradox is usually presented, as Forster presents it here, as if it were a truism.[1]

Prudery and reticence, then, as to sex or death: the Bloomsbury writer Forster shares with his evangelical Protestant forebears these odd Victorian attitudes, but applies them to death rather than sex, defying the old taboo with early diffidence, but boldly enough in the later fiction, while tacitly observing the new one. So too—though Cockshut fails to make the connection—does Virginia Woolf. Death is an omnipresent subject in her fiction, but in spite of—or rather because of—its enormous importance, she confines it to parentheses, as in *To the Lighthouse*, averts it through sleep or trances, as in *Orlando*, or consigns it to another country, as in *Jacob's Room* and *The Waves*, or to a scapegoat double, as in *Mrs. Dalloway*; whereas sex is a subject which she deals with more straightforwardly, more openly, though (as we shall see) not without tempering restraint. But death is decidedly the more troubling dominion for her.

There are in fact only two deathbed scenes in her fiction. The first, in her first novel, *The Voyage Out* (1915), involves a young woman like herself, Rachel Vinrace, whose dying reveries reflect her own early breakdowns and prefigure her attempted suicide shortly after finishing the novel. The second, in her late popular novel, *The Years* (1937), involves a Victorian mother like her own, Rose Pargiter, whose angry daughter Delia resents her prolonged illness and is all too relieved at her passing. As we shall see, Virginia Woolf was herself unable to grieve at her mother's deathbed when she was thirteen, for richer and more interesting causes than any reflected by these overcharged fictional occasions; and she was alternately relieved and overwhelmed with grief by her father's death when she was twenty-two. Her breakdowns after each of these events testify to their enormous importance for her, and by the same token, to their potential importance for us. For her personal ordeals help to explain the emergence in our time of a new prohibition, a new taboo on the tender emotions of grief and loss. Like the novelist Bernard in *The Waves*, we too "have no ceremonies" with which to mourn our beloved dead, "only private dirges and no conclusions, only violent sensations, each separate"; and we may well want to agree with him that "nothing that has been said meets our case" (*TW*, p. 157). Our own refusals to mourn owe much, moreover, to the transition from late-Victorian effusiveness to modern prudery and reticence which Virginia Woolf and others like her have made for us. Her quarrel with grieving is very much our quarrel, and as such, very much the justification for this study.

The forthright title of her famous essay "The Captain's Death Bed" might seem to contradict these conclusions. But the essay itself confirms them by focusing on the rarity, for her as for us, of a tranquil and meaningful death. It opens with a description of Frederick Marryat, a sea captain and the author of "a long shelf of books of adventure," as he lies dying one August morning in 1848 in a cheerful room with mirrored doors, a ceiling painted like the sky, and walls decorated with painted birds on roses. When his loving daughter brings him a bouquet of flowers, Marryat dictates to her this final testament:

> 'Tis a lovely day and Augusta has just brought me three pinks and three roses, and the bouquet is charming. I have opened the windows and the air is delightful. It is now exactly nine o'clock in the morning, and I am lying in a bed in a place called Langham, two miles from the sea, on the coast of Norfolk. . . . To use the common sense of the word I am happy. I have no sense of hunger whatever, or of thirst; my taste is not impaired. . . . After years of casual, and, latterly, months of intense thought, I feel convinced that Christianity is true . . . and that God is love. . . . It is now half-past nine o'clock. World, adieu. [*CE* 1:173]

Virginia Woolf's fascination with this "dying man whose thoughts turned to love and roses as he lay among his looking-glasses and his painted roses" is easy to explain: he is dying the kind of death she wanted for her atheistic and self-centered father; a mid-Victorian death before the inroads of doubt rendered the funereal effusions of her late-Victorian relatives so suspect; a dignified straightforward death which made her father's previous

effusions over her dead mother, and his own unbearably protracted dying, seem shameful by comparison. The loving daughter
is, by the same tokens, an idyllic version of herself, saying with
flowers what she felt she had failed to say to her dying father. She
can write about this death, then, because it appeals to admiration
rather than shame, and because it answers all the questions about
faith, love, flowering and creative life, that she could not answer
for herself, no more than we have managed to answer them for
ourselves in our own related time. It is the absence of this serenity
and self-acceptance that she wants to share with us, like a lost
hope or faith.

Her own sense of futility at Hardy's funeral in 1928 (WD, p.
122), and of nullity at the funerals of friends and literary peers, are
further signs of absent sustenance. The recent publication of letters, memoirs, and diaries studded with such occasions brings into
bold relief the problem of her own inability to grieve and its
importance for her fiction. And here too her frequent commemorative "lives" should be cited, for she was something of a
specialist in restrained obituaries.[2] It is in fact the rich potential of
such material which moved me to pursue this study. Though the
importance of death in her fiction has often been noted, no one
has made much of the absence of grief, or of that characteristic
difficulty with grieving, that she shares with her contemporaries.
An instance of the more general modern taboo on tenderness, it
deserves to be studied in itself wherever correlations of life and
literature can tell us something about its origins and consequences. And here the life and works of Virginia Woolf decidedly
meet our case.

Most recent attempts to correlate Woolf's life and art derive
from Quentin Bell's *Virginia Woolf: A Biography* (1972) and
from the astonishing round of scholarship it set in motion. Publications appearing within the last few years include the first five
volumes of a complete edition of her letters; the first three volumes of a complete edition of her diaries; her unpublished autobiographical writings, *Moments of Being* (1976); her father's
family recollections, *The Mausoleum Book* (1977); a selection of

unreprinted literary and biographical essays, *Books and Portraits* (1977); the unpublished novel-essay chapters of *The Years*, called *The Pargiters* (1977); a manuscript edition of *The Waves* (1976); her unpublished play for Bloomsbury friends, *Freshwater: A Comedy* (1976); and her uncollected Dalloway stories, *Mrs. Dalloway's Party* (1973). Along with Bell's impressive findings and Leonard Woolf's earlier memoirs, these new autobiographical and literary documents allow for correlations of the life and works on a scale hitherto unimagined. Thus Jean O. Love (*Virginia Woolf: Sources of Madness and Art*, 1977), Phyllis Rose (*Woman of Letters: A Life of Virginia Woolf*, 1978), and Roger Poole (*The unknown Virginia Woolf*, 1978) are able to speculate in far greater depth than Bell on the author's troubled childhood, her early difficulties in marriage, her lesbian leanings and her feminist liberation, and their bearing on her literary achievement. Such psychological correlations are always risky, but as early as 1928, in her introduction to the Modern Library edition of *Mrs. Dalloway*, Virginia Woolf herself had provided the rationale for pursuing them:

> It is true that the author can if he wishes tell us something about himself and his life which is not in the novel; and to this effort we should do all that we can to encourage him. For nothing is more fascinating than to be shown the truth which lies behind those immense façades of fiction—if life is indeed true, and if fiction is indeed fictitious. And probably the connection between the two is highly complicated. Books are the flowers or fruit stuck here and there on a tree which has its roots deep down in the earth of our earliest life, of our first experiences. But here again to tell the reader anything that his own imagination and insight have not already discovered would need not a page or two of preface but a volume or two of autobiography. Slowly and cautiously one would have to go to work, uncovering, laying bare, and even so when everything had been brought to the surface, it would still be for the reader to decide what was relevant and what not. [pp. v–vi]

A member of the Memoir Club from "Old Bloomsbury," and of a family addicted to memoirs, Virginia Woolf had done much of the uncovering of her own first experiences in the essays

6

now happily collected and published in *Moments of Being*. Particularly in "A Sketch of the Past," started in April 1939 and continued until four months before her death in 1941, she had tried to piece together her impressions from childhood and adolescence of those personal and familial experiences which help to explain her madness and her art; and she had done so with the same fascinated regard for the fictions of life, and the truths of fiction, the same slow caution, the same modesty as to relevance, that she called for in her 1928 remarks. It is not surprising, then, that scholars like Love, Rose, and Poole have taken her at her word, and have based their books on her hitherto unavailable recollections.

This study is a further speculation on "what was relevant and what not" in Virginia Woolf's memoirs. It begins with a chapter on the most baffling childhood episode, her deathbed reactions in 1895 when she had secretly laughed at her mother's crying nurse and, on a second visit, had hallucinated a man at the edge of her mother's bed. Her recollection of these strange events came slowly and imperfectly—a brief blurred glimpse of the first visit in 1924, while she was writing *Mrs. Dalloway*; a somewhat sharper but still imperfect version of the same visit in 1934, while she was writing *The Years*; and a full sequential clarification in "A Sketch of the Past" in 1939. As this gradual and erratic sorting out suggests, she was dealing with painfully blocked emotions. Her lifelong quarrel with grieving must have begun with that impaction, and her madness may have begun there too, for as Helene Deutsch has shown, "absence of grief" usually proceeds from an emotional conflict which demands resolution, and which can persist for a lifetime unless it is resolved.[3]

The personal and literary ramifications of Virginia's absent grief, and of that curious hallucination which seems to explain it, are what interests me. Let me say straight off what I develop at some length in the next chapter: I believe that the hallucinated man (whom Virginia never identifies) was Julia Stephen's deceased first husband, Herbert Duckworth, to whom in Virginia's fantasy her mother had returned after eight years of widowhood and seventeen years of marriage to Virginia's father; and that her mother's seeming desertion of the family for this long-lost ghost—the source in life of her private sorrows and of her continuing widowhood even through her second marriage—was the secret cause of Virginia's scornful laughter. From this working hypothesis I draw several speculative conclusions. One is that Julia Stephen's ghostly repossession became the model for Virginia's repossessions by parental ghosts over the next thirty-two years, until by writing *To the Lighthouse* she was finally able to dispel (or at least disperse) their daily visitations. Another is that her mother's conviction of the senselessness of death, which began with her own widowing, became Virginia's conviction at thirteen, reinforced by the impaction of her own tangled feelings, by the ensuing funereal gloom which further repressed her feelings (as I discuss in chapter 3), and by three more deaths in the family over the next eleven years. A third speculative conclusion is that the passionate love which her undemonstrative mother withheld from Leslie Stephen, and which she reserved in Virginia's fantasy for her patient ghostly lover, became the model for the passion Virginia too withheld from all living men, gave only fleetingly to living women, and similarly reserved for her own beloved ghosts. Thus her lifelong inability to love—to achieve anything like richly passionate fulfillment—seems to have been peculiarly intertwined with her lifelong inability to grieve; and the neglected Duckworth legend—along with the now famous triflings of Duckworth's surviving sons—goes a long way toward explaining that apparent entanglement.

Let me pause to compare these initial speculations with those of Bell, Love, Rose, and Poole. None of them deal with the Duckworth legend nor with Virginia's deathbed hallucination nor with the possible connections between them; and only Rose deals directly (and even then briefly) with Virginia's secret laughter. So none of them reach the above conclusions. Nevertheless they all contribute to my working hypothesis in what seem to me exciting ways. Quentin Bell provides indispensable and exact information about Virginia's four major breakdowns and two attempted suicides between 1895 and 1915—something which no other scholar has done. Jean Love helpfully shows that Virginia felt deprived of her mother's love even before her untimely death, that she had not advanced by then much beyond her preoedipal attachment in early infancy; and to this end she cites too early weaning because of her mother's poor health, the distraction in her first year of life of a backward sister (Laura) needing her mother's attention, displacement by a younger favorite (Adrian) in her second year, and those frequent charitable sorties outside the home, to the neglect of all her children, for which Julia Stephen was famous. Along with this convincing rationale for early and excessive dependency, Love also shows how Virginia later tried ineffectually to mourn her mother's loss through neurotic attachments to older women and through daily hallucinations of her mother's presence.[4] In her brief assessment of Virginia's absent grief Phyllis Rose provides a theory which allows us to trace such prolonged difficulties to a peculiar form of arrested adolescence: for if adolescence itself is "a kind of extended mourning, a gradual detachment from the parents who have been until then major objects of love," then Virginia would have missed that gradual initiation into loss which makes possible the actual work of mourning when parents die in later years—and this does help to explain her long imperfect mourning of an all too early loss.[5] Roger Poole provides a similarly useful view of Virginia's second major breakdown after her father's death in 1904, when the effect of her half brother George Duckworth's increasingly erotic attentions while her father lay dying was to repeat the pattern of death and defilement which contributed (as I try to show though Poole does not) to her initial breakdown in 1895.[6] And finally, in *A Literature of Their Own*, still another correlating scholar, Elaine Showalter, helpfully suggests that Virginia's symptoms during and after her first breakdown are like those which often accompany the onset of unusually severe menstruation in adolescent girls, and may well have established her lifelong connection of femaleness with death.[7]

Elsewhere I have discussed my several differences with Love, Rose, and Poole at some length,[8] and they will surface at appropriate points in the pages and footnotes ahead. But meanwhile the interconnections between our varied speculations seem to me significant, for they indicate that we approach the novels themselves with the same sense of deeply felt problems reflected in them or excluded from them, and with considerable agreement as to what those problems are. Indeed, the emergence of a converging rather than conflicting body of ideas about such matters—as in the instances garnered above—promises to bring the novels closer to us, if only by disclosing their all too human sources. But as every psychological critic knows, the disclosures extend to the novels themselves—to choices and rejections, themes and preoccupations, weaknesses and strengths, which inform their pages and which can only be accounted for by speculations on the author's life. My own intention is to use such speculations to illuminate two major novels, *Mrs. Dalloway* and *To the Lighthouse*, in which Virginia Woolf first wrestles in earnest with her entangled love and grief, and almost disentangles them. Her near-successes here seem to me more interesting, more humanly meaningful, than her assured successes elsewhere; and for that reason my study of her lifelong quarrel with grieving will concentrate on these novels, or more accurately, on the near-solution to that quarrel which she reaches through them and on the textual weaknesses which betray her partial failure.

In *Mrs. Dalloway*, for instance, Woolf begins to write a novel in which she openly confronts the problem of impacted grief in a woman much like herself; but, changing her original intention, she deliberately shifts this burden from the woman to a suicidal double—and then further obscures her original intention by blaming the double's obtuse neurologists for his suicide and by drawing from his defiance of those neurologists a wishful and vicarious redemption for her untouched heroine. In *To the Lighthouse*, however, Woolf returns to the childhood sources of her own blocked grief and successfully conveys the release of impacted feelings in a young spinster woman like herself; but, to avoid sentimentality and confusion, she circumvents the death which created that impaction, oversimplifies the life histories of her major characters, and so leaves untouched the most secret causes for her initial inability to grieve.

These authorial choices and evasions seem to me legitimate matter for critical speculation; they reveal an ongoing struggle with her material in which the author's emotional involvement and authority are profoundly at stake, and therefore open to critical judgment. Though the risk of confusion and misjudgment is great, it is a risk worth taking if—as I believe—it illuminates major texts, helps us to appraise their strengths and weaknesses, and extends our literary grasp of significant human problems.

In my next chapter and at other points I will use most of the other novels to advance these speculations. It would be possible to demonstrate their elegiac dimensions at some length, as Phyllis Rose has demonstrated their feminist dimensions. But to do so would be to dwell on the evasions of a writer who is not wholly engaged with her inmost problems. In her first novel, *The Voyage Out*, for instance, the love between heroine and hero is shown at the end to be more complete in death than it ever was in life, and the surviving hero accordingly feels no need to grieve his lost beloved. Indeed, like Virginia at her mother's deathbed, he at first feels "nothing at all" (*VO*, p. 357). But then, sitting at the edge of the heroine's bed like Virginia's hallucinated ghost, he begins to feel the "perfect happiness" of their selfless bodiless union— "the union which had been impossible while they lived" (*VO*, pp. 358–59); and so he speaks aloud the words which, as it happens, Virginia's mother reserved for her marriage to Herbert Duckworth:"No two people have ever been so happy as we have been" (*VO*, p. 359; *MB*, pp. 32, 89). In this euphoric state he is pushed from the room by unknown hands, until he realizes that he will not see his beloved in this world again and, crying out her name in anguish, tries to rush back into the bedroom—even as Leslie Stephen had rushed *out* of his dead wife's room in 1895, past Virginia's outstretched arms, crying out something she "could not catch" (*MB*, p. 91). The scene is an amalgam, then, of deathbed memories and obsessions in which Virginia plays her mother's part, receives in death the serene yet anguished love of Duckworth-Stephen, and so avoids the actual marriage with Leonard Woolf which now threatens to engulf her. After attempting suicide within six months of the novel's completion, and after one year of marriage, she would never again present such a naive version of her secret yearnings and evasions.

Phyllis Rose argues that Virginia Woolf earns this arbitrary death by portraying the dying heroine's reveries with enormous power; but as she also recognizes, the illness so effectively conveyed is mental rather than physical—"the ultimate room of her own"—for which deathly union is the dreamlike cure.[9] Woolf would move to the other extreme in her late novel *The Years*, where her feminist liberation leads to harsher and supposedly more "realistic" attitudes. Thus Delia Pargiter unfeelingly rejects her slowly dying mother and dreams of a surrogate union with her father, who in turn visits his mistress as his wife expires. As I hope to show in later chapters, this near-parody of the classic Freudian triangle is as falsely conceived as the idealized death in *The Voyage Out*. One portion of this novel will prove useful, however, in helping me to identify "the robber in the bedroom" in the chapter ahead; and in my final chapter, my assessment of *The Pargiters*—the original novel-essay version of *The Years*—will help me to establish the divided (hence somewhat shaky) nature of Woolf's feminist rebellion.

The elegies to Virginia's dead brother Thoby, in *Jacob's Room* and *The Waves*, are technically more effective than *The Years*; but these experimental fictions suffer nonetheless from an emotional vacancy beneath their surface brilliance, a failure to evoke their subject with anything like the force of Mrs. Ramsay's presence in *To the Lighthouse*; and for that deficiency there are no technical compensations. Virginia loved and mourned her brother Thoby; but she did not know him well, nor mourn him to the point of madness, and could not draw upon her strong obsessions in portraying him. He is always more of an absence than a presence, and though her very methods are an anguished reaching after absence, what they chiefly grasp—for this reader at least—is vacancy.

As I have already indicated, there are evasions too in *Mrs. Dalloway* and *To the Lighthouse*; but in these impressive novels the engagement with entangled love and grief is more direct, and the evasions help to secure that engagement by circumventing emotional impediments, like the painful connection between absent grief and suicide, or the painfulness of the death scene which first impacted grief. In these novels, moreover, Virginia Woolf will attempt to sort out her childhood confusions about passionate, companionate, and predatory love; and though she will not dispel those confusions, she will at least break through to her own spinsterly independence from parental ghosts. In *Mrs. Dalloway* she will falsely approach such independence through vicarious suicide; but her failure here will act like a reprieve, an assurance of survival while she makes her more direct bid for independence in *To the Lighthouse*; and that sequential achievement may explain why strong independent spinsters, married or unmarried, male or female or both, will dominate the later fiction, as with Bernard in *The Waves*, Eleanor in *The Years*, Miss La Trobe in *Between the Acts*, and the bisexual Orlando.

Spinsterly independence, whether in characters or authors, may seem like an odd achievement; but when we compare it with Leopold Bloom's curious abstinence in *Ulysses*, or Jake Barnes's unmanned stoicism in *The Sun Also Rises*, or Strether's cultivated innocence in *The Ambassadors*, it takes its place among modern modes of isolate survival. From *Ulysses* Virginia Woolf would also draw inspiration for stream-of-consciousness devices in *Mrs. Dalloway* and *To the Lighthouse* which both express that isolation and bring her closer to its secret causes; and she would use the cemetery scene in *Ulysses*, and perhaps the remorse at another deathbed defiance which grips that novel's artist-hero, as precedents for investigating those causes. For at the heart of these sequential novels there is the same nexus of ungrieved grief, and of troubled parental relations, as in Joyce's emotional odyssey.

It should be clear at this point that Woolf's last memoir, "A Sketch of the Past," is at the heart of my own odyssean speculations. In my next chapter I subject it to the most searching explication it has yet received; and if I use it to refresh and amplify our comprehension of well-known fictions, I also use those fictions to elicit its refreshing power. So "A Sketch of the Past" is the third and perhaps the most important text on which this study concentrates, an unfinished work of art itself, and the most courageous of the author's many probings into childhood problems. As I indicate in my final chapter, moreover, Virginia Woolf achieved a measure of serenity from this courageous venture which she wanted to share with others. She wanted these childhood revelations to be shared, pondered, and related to her fiction. Though she had strong feelings about the invasion of privacy, and resisted professional analysis, she was nonetheless willing as her life drew near its close to conduct her own investigations with an eye to their eventual publication. In other words, she was herself a psycho-literary speculator and a believer, however posthumously, in the universal interest of all such inquiries.

That interest lies, I think, in tracing the curve of a writer's career—what Norman Mailer calls "the pilgrimage . . . the life . . . [the] emotional odyssey"[10]—so as to reveal and conserve its human costs and consequences, its heroic and pathetic ranges, its more poignant human dimensions. This is not to reduce art to human frailties, as some insist, but to restore some sense of the human struggle by which it rises into being. Admittedly, my own investigation of Woolf's extensive struggle is limited in length, but not I hope in speculative scope and boldness nor in focused concentration on essential problems and their literary resolutions. What I have tried for, in any case, is a synoptic assessment of the author's brave, ongoing, and ultimately tragic attempt to come to terms with the senselessness of the many deaths she endured from childhood onward, and with such probing frightened honesty as to make her private quarrel with grief and loss our common public quarrel.

One final cautionary note before my synoptic odyssey begins: much of the material of Woolf's childhood and adolescence which appears in the next two chapters will be familiar to readers of recent Woolf studies; but since I place it in a different light and reach new and original conclusions about its literary and personal relevance, my approach should reanimate and extend its almost legendary interest for our time.

2 The Robber in the Bedroom; or, The Thief of Love

The light being dim, it was impossible to see any change in her face. An immense feeling of peace came over Terence, so that he had no wish to move or to speak. The terrible torture and unreality of the last days were over, and he had come out now into perfect certainty and peace. His mind began to work naturally again and with great ease. The longer he sat there the more profoundly was he conscious of the peace invading every corner of his soul. Once he held his breath and listened acutely; she was still breathing; he went on thinking for some time; they seemed to be thinking together; he seemed to be Rachel as well as himself; and then he listened again; no, she had ceased to breathe. So much the better—this was death. It was nothing; it was to cease to breathe. It was happiness, it was perfect happiness. They had now what they had always wanted to have, the union which had been impossible while they lived. Unconscious, whether he thought the words or spoke them aloud, he said, 'No two people have ever been so happy as we have been. No one has ever loved as we have loved.'

It seemed to him that their complete union and happiness filled the room with rings eddying more and more widely. He had no wish in the world left unfulfilled. They possessed what could never be taken from them.

The Voyage Out (pp. 358–59)

On May 5, 1924, on the twenty-ninth anniversary of her mother's death, Virginia Woolf would write in her diary that she "could fill a whole page & more" with her impressions of that bygone day, "many of them ill received by me, & hidden from the grown ups, but very memorable on that account: how I laughed, for instance, behind the hand which was meant to hide my tears; & through the fingers saw the nurses sobbing." She would then break off—"But enough of death—its life that matters"—without explaining why she laughed or at what (*DVW* 2:300–301). Fifteen years would elapse before she would actually fill that "page & more" with "memorable" impressions of her mother's death, and of her own preceding life, which help to explain her secret laughter. Meanwhile, some ten years later, she would attempt her first articulate probing of that strange reaction and its elusive causes. Thus, in her diary entry for September 12, 1934, the sobbing nurses of 1924—seen *while* she hides her laughter—become a single crying nurse *at* whose supposed insincerity she laughs, as if to defend her own deficient feeling: "Remember turning aside at mother's bed, when she was dead, and Stella [her half sister] took us in, to laugh, secretly, at the nurse crying. She's pretending, I said, aged 13, and was afraid I was not feeling enough. So now" (*WD*, pp. 223–24).

She had been reminded again of this moment by the death of an old friend, Roger Fry, and by her dazed, wooden response to the prospect of attending his funeral; and she had framed the moment with a quotation from Maupassant on the artist's temperament, his compulsive need to analyze and observe rather than respond simply and freshly to experience. But whether in 1924 or 1934, the response recalled seems fresh enough: she *laughs* at her mother's deathbed—a reaction so inappropriate that she hides it from the grownups, and so disturbing in its *definite* expression that she conflates it with its opposite—an insufficiency of appropriate feeling—and assigns it, even in retrospect, to the artist's compulsive and unfeeling need to watch and analyze.

Whether in her life or in her work, however, this difficulty with grieving recurs too often, and too insistently, to be passed off as a matter of artistic temperament. Its presence in her experimental fiction—the elegies for her dead brother Thoby in *Jacob's Room* and *The Waves*, the elegy for her dead mother in *To the Lighthouse*, the taboo on grieving in *Mrs. Dalloway*—suggests rather a compulsive need to cope with death. Indeed, while writing *To the Lighthouse* she had even thought of supplanting "novel" as the name for her books with something like "elegy" (*WD*, p. 80). Perhaps "abortive elegies for our times" would be more appropriate, since she refuses in these books to deal with death and grieving in any direct or open way, and her elegiac impulse—by which writer and reader alike may normally work out grief through formal measures—is delayed, disguised, or thwarted—at best only partially appeased. Her refusal seems to me characteristic of our times, or of that struggle against Victorian odds which helped to make our times, and I want to speculate accordingly on its private derivations.

Given this license to delve into biography, we may still want to take her recollections at face value, and to assess her secret laughter at the crying nurse (or nurses) as a normal childhood suspicion that adults are faking their feelings. But the suspicion has been "normal" only since Victorian times, when children first acquired their mythical edge on adults in naturalness and freshness of feeling; and we have no reason in any case to believe that the nurse was (or the nurses were) faking.[1] Or we may want to assess it as a temporary aberration on an awesome, even frightening occasion, an embarrassed evasion of some expected grownup response which the child can't make; and of course she does dwell on grownup expectations in her brief recollections of 1924 and 1934 (though not, as we shall see, in their modest 1939 expansion). But this charged and erratic memory was released successively over a fifteen-year period, some thirty to forty-five years after the event, as if by gradual defusion; it was an event, moreover, to which she repeatedly returned in her fiction, her diaries, and her autobiographical writings, as if trying to exhaust its painfulness. Then too, her first serious breakdown, soon after her mother's death, lends weight to the slender recollections and allows us to pose a set of modern psychoanalytic questions we might otherwise eschew. Why, after all, was she unable to feel enough at this crisis, unable, apparently, to cry? Did she want her mother to die, as some Freudians might conjecture, and was she therefore secretly pleased (and later overcome by guilt) when life granted her wish? Or was she angry with her mother for dying, for depriving her of love, and—converting that response into defensive scorn for the crying nurse—was she then unable to grieve (and later overcome by guilt), as still other Freudians, like Helene Deutsch, or counter-Freudians like Ian Suttie, might argue?[2] Though there is much evidence for the first view, and though I once held it myself, I am going to be pressing now for the Deutsch and Suttie view because I believe it accounts more inclusively for the biographical facts, for their cultural implications, and most importantly, for their relation to Woolf's fictive approaches to such problems. At stake here, I might add, is the ongoing debate as to whether the preoedipal bond in infancy was stronger in Woolf's case than the oedipal or "elektral" rivalries which supposedly succeeded it—an issue which, for psychoanalytic critics at least, can radically affect the way one sees her life and work.[3]

Consider in this light the frequency with which she not only brings her mother back to life in her fictions, but, in literal or spiritual ways, extends her lifeline. The portrait of Mrs. Ramsay in *To the Lighthouse* is the famous instance, to which we will return; but it is only one of a series of such resurrections and extensions. In her first novel, *The Voyage Out* (1915), the young heroine, Rachel Vinrace, is chaperoned by an aunt and uncle, Helen and Ridley Ambrose, during her stay in South America. The Ambroses seem to me largely modeled upon the author's parents, Julia and Leslie Stephen. Ridley is, like Leslie, a blunt scholar and spoiled husband who insults or embarrasses others openly, depends on his wife to arrange things for him, and retires from all complications to his scholarly work. Helen, like Julia, is a beautiful loving woman, anxious about her children, deferential to her husband, profoundly troubled by life's senseless disasters and hence determinedly agnostic, and—above all—deeply interested in others in protective ways and much given to deciding their fates.[4] In the course of the "voyage out" to South America, for instance, on a ship captained by her brother Willoughby, who is also Rachel's father, Helen decides that her niece Rachel needs her supervision. As indeed she does. Her mother having died when she was eleven, Rachel has been left in the care of spinster aunts and, like most Victorian children, raised in abysmal ignorance of sexual realities. Her father, who is equally blind to such matters, wants to bring her up now "as her mother would have wished," and speaks of using her as his hostess and companion while he works his way toward Parliament through social contacts. In his affectionate selfishness he is modeled upon Virginia Woolf's half brother George Duckworth, who took it upon himself to raise the Stephen children after the deaths of Julia Duckworth Stephen and her oldest daughter, Stella Duckworth; and who then used Virginia and her older sister Vanessa as hostesses and companions to further his own social ambitions. He also seems to have made at least enthymematic love to them (with one step left out), a role which is diverted in the novel from Willoughby to Richard Dalloway, another "pompous and sentimental" man (as Helen pointedly types him), who tries to make love to Rachel, to her surprise and terror, on the "voyage out."[5] In the novel, then, Rachel is rescued from her creator's fate by Helen Ambrose, who sees her need for guidance, decides to take charge of her education, and so saves her from the kind of sexual and social exploitation her creator suffered.

Virginia Woolf's fictive choices here are, I think, biographically telling. She has put her dead mother's replacement in a position to give her heroine the kind of support and guidance she was herself deprived of by her mother's death. She has shown thereby—and in the most heartfelt way—how much she wanted her mother to live, how much she missed her nurturing presence. There is much private poignance, then, in Helen's recognition of Rachel's sexual ignorance and of her father's exploitive ways, in her placement of the Dalloway episode for her, in her determination to rouse her from romantic self-absorption, in her diversion of the wrong analytic suitor (St. John Hirst) while the right intuitive one (Terence Hewet) proposes, and in her dreamlike sanction then of the coming marriage, her reluctant withdrawal from guardianship, and her helpless premonitions of approaching disaster. For even this resurrected mother cannot save Rachel from that Victorian heritage, senseless death, by which her virginity and her independence are alike preserved on the eve of marriage. Virginia Woolf's attempted suicide not long after the novel's completion, and barely a year after her marriage to Leonard Woolf, may help to explain her decision to wipe out Rachel and her odd fictive means for doing it: a mysterious fever contracted, apparently, while sealing her engagement in a dreamlike embrace upon a womblike Amazon jungle floor. The sexual and emotional strains of marriage must have brought Virginia close to the original complex tensions of her mother's senseless death, and she could bring Julia back to life only by the imagined sacrifice of someone like herself to the same senseless forces.

For convenience I am going to limit myself now to certain

essential points about the next four novels so as to focus on the
more useful details of the last novel in my speculative sequence,
The Years. In her second novel, then, *Night and Day* (1919), we
need only note that the maternal counselor, Maggie Hilbery, is a
vague, ineffectual, literary lady whom Virginia Woolf based on
her aunt Lady Anny Ritchie, whose career as a novelist might be
said to sanction her own budding career;[6] that Mrs. Hilbery is
more her daughter's ward than her guiding light through most of
the novel; but that she takes charge of things at the end, dispels her
daughter's romantic vacillations, quiets her flustered husband,
and much more grandly than Helen Ambrose, sanctions a life-
directed marriage by speaking wisely for faith in love against her
daughter's fear of finding it an illusion. With this act of effective
maternal guidance, moreover, her daughter interestingly finds
extraordinary pleasure in being able to talk thus freely to someone
"equally wise and equally benignant," someone whom she then
identifies as *"the mother of her earliest childhood, whose silences seemed to answer questions that were never asked"* (italics
mine). At the decisive point, then, Mrs. Hilbery becomes another
Julia Stephen.

In her next novel, *Jacob's Room* (1922), Virginia Woolf
returns to the real Julia Stephen for her maternal model, choosing
her years of widowhood after her first husband's death when she
had to raise three children by herself, but focusing her maternal
concern on a child of her second marriage, Thoby Stephen, who as
Jacob Flanders is designed to die in Flanders fields. The extension
of her mother's lifeline through World War I, and the ostensible
removal of her father from the fictive scene, are the interesting
points here; for in this first experiment in impressionistic and
poetic fiction the mother's role is sharply limited: she exists only
to comfort, praise, and worry about her three sons, mourn her
dead husband, discourage eligible suitors out of love for him, and
so react with bravery and cheer to her lonely widowed lot. As the
novel begins her husband is two years dead from refusing to
change his boots after his duck's worth of duckshooting,[7] and she
hears his voice in every tolling funeral bell; as the novel closes she
holds up a pair of her dead son Jacob's shoes and asks his friend
Bonamy, "What am I to do with these?" The unspoken answer

seems to be to defy death's senselessness by giving vigorous life-witness to it, as Julia Stephen did—not incidentally—through her deep and continuing attachment to her dead first husband, Herbert Duckworth.

In her next experimental novel, *Mrs. Dalloway* (1925), where the adoption of stream-of-consciousness techniques brings the author closer to subjective realities, there are—surprisingly—no parental figures. But Mrs. Dalloway herself is endowed with many of Julia Stephen's traits, including her capacity to enjoy life intensely *because of*, rather than in spite of, her stoic atheism; and her young sacrificial double, Septimus Warren Smith, is given a de facto role like that of Rachel Vinrace in *The Voyage Out*, in that he commits suicide so that the fifty-year-old Mrs. Dalloway may live—may experience that defiant fate vicariously, that is, and so learn to face and embrace life bravely after her frightening bout with influenza (the disease, incidentally, which killed Julia Stephen at about the same age). The sacrificial Smith's insanity and suicide are connected, moreover, with the death of an older superior officer and friend, a man named Evans, whom he has failed to mourn; and his inability to feel in this instance, to grieve his dead older friend, is the chief crime for which he feels himself condemned to death. Plainly Virginia Woolf was getting closer in this novel to the sources of her own bouts with insanity and of her own suicidal impulses: and it is no accident that she deals more directly and effectively with these sources in her next novel, *To the Lighthouse* (1927), in which her fictive resurrections of Julia Stephen might be said to culminate, and in which her parents are treated for the first time as protagonists rather than supporting characters.

She believed at first that she was writing this book about her father, chiefly, and that the relief she gained from writing it, to which my remarks here will be confined, might also be attributed to him. Thus, writing in her diary on November 28, 1928, on what would have been her father's ninety-sixth birthday, she felt again the relief of his death in 1904, the release to her life's work it enabled, for, quite interestingly, it was not her mother, but her father, *whom she did not want to live*; and so she says now that his life, if extended, "would have entirely ended mine. What would

have happened? No writing, no books—inconceivable." And then, more tellingly:

> I used to think of him and mother daily; but writing the *Lighthouse* laid them in my mind. And now he comes back sometimes, but differently. (I believe this to be true—that I was obsessed by them both, unhealthily; and writing of them was a necessary act.) He comes back now more as a contemporary. I must read him some day. I wonder if I can feel again, I hear his voice, I know this by heart? [*WD*, p. 138]

Actually she would continue to think of both parents, and to write about them, to the end of her days, and the question of her capacity to "feel again," raised so unintelligibly here about her father's presence, would be crucial to her recurring obsession. Yet there is no doubt that writing *To the Lighthouse* relieved her immensely. Returning to that theme in 1939, and this time focusing more accurately on her mother as the more central presence in her life, she tried to explain the sudden dimming of that tutelary spirit:

> Until I was in the forties . . . the presence of my mother obsessed me. I could hear her voice, see her, imagine what she would do or say as I went about my day's doings. She was one of the invisible presences who after all play so important a part in every life. . . . It is perfectly true that she obsessed me, in spite of the fact that she died when I was thirteen, until I was forty-four. Then one day walking around Tavistock Square I made up, as I sometimes make up my books, *To the Lighthouse*; in a great, apparently involuntary, rush. . . . I wrote the book very quickly; and when it was written, I ceased to be obsessed by my mother. I no longer hear her voice; I do not see her.
> I suppose that I did for myself what psychoanalysts do for their patients. I expressed some very long felt and deeply felt emotion. And in expressing it I explained it and then laid it to rest. But what is the meaning of 'explained' it? Why, because I described her and my feeling for her in that book, should my vision of her and my feeling for her become so much dimmer and weaker? Perhaps one of these days I shall hit on the reason; and if so, I will give it. [*MB*, pp. 80–81]

What she had worked out in *To the Lighthouse*, in a powerful if partial way, was the burden of unexpressed grief, guilt, and anger from her childhood experience of her mother's death. As Helene Deutsch argues, the absence of grief on such occasions leaves undone the normal work of mourning—the need to work through the sense of loss, to let go of the lost love, the lost person, by expressing unadmitted love, and to reinvest that love once more in the living, or in what Woolf calls "life itself."[8] What Woolf describes here, then, is the long-delayed work of mourning, the letting go of the lost mother through expressive grief and love, the dimming of her presence as Woolf turns once more to life. And yet—perhaps because she avoids the actual death scene and represses so much else in *To the Lighthouse*—she never wholly freed herself from the burden of these years. In her most popular novel, *The Years* (1937), and in the "Sketch of the Past" from which I have just quoted, which she worked on until four months before her suicide in 1941, she returned to them again as if to complete her all too partial therapy.

In some ways *The Years* represents her most heroic fictive effort to put old ghosts to rest. There is first of all the decided dimming of Julia Stephen's presence. Cast as a dying woman, Rose Pargiter, as the novel opens in 1880 (so that she dies, in effect, even before Virginia Woolf is born), she is briefly glimpsed among the bedclothes, immersed in "the private world of illness," wandering endlessly and vaguely "in this borderland between life and death." If her sudden cry, "Where am I?" is repeated by her children throughout their lives, her own whereabouts is confined for the rest of the novel to her photograph as a white-robed girl with a flower basket; and, to the family waiting for her death, that photograph is more vivid even now than her dying presence.

Secondly, there is the actual death scene—a rarity in Woolf's fiction—which seems at first glance to come remarkably close to her childhood experience and to explain its hidden meaning. Thus the mother's protracted dying has made at least one of her daughters, Delia, savagely angry. She longs for her mother's death, feels joy at signs of her weakness, despairs when she recovers a little strength, sees her mother's obstinate clinging

to life as an impediment to her own existence. Nor is she able to grieve at any time, though she repeatedly tries to feel affection, pity, anything at all. She believes, moreover, that her father, Colonel Pargiter, feels as she does about this overwhelming illness, by which the whole family is paralyzed, and will not mourn his wife's eventual death. When in fact he stumbles out of his dead wife's room, crying her name passionately, arms outstretched, fists clenched, Delia (like Virginia with the sobbing nurse or nurses) can only take his grief as artful pretense: "You did that very well, she told him as he passed her. It was like a scene from a play" (*TY*, p. 38).

At least one Freudian critic cites this sequence as evidence of the "childish sense of rivalry for her father's love" which would account for Woolf's inability to grieve her mother's death;[9] and I myself applied that view for many years to the mourning problems in *Mrs. Dalloway* and *To the Lighthouse*. Certainly *The Years* seems to support it. Delia's romantic fantasies about Parnell, for instance, may be seen as a projection of her attachment to her father, whose visit to his mistress while his wife is dying in 1880 anticipates the scandal of 1889, when Parnell's relations with Kitty O'Shea were first revealed. In this light Delia's alignment with her father, her desire to get rid of his dying wife so as to become "Parnell's" beloved, seem set before us like pieces of an oedipal puzzle. Later in the novel Woolf even attributes oedipal love to the spinster doctor, Peggy Pargiter, the daughter of Delia's brother Morris, in Delia's presence.

The trouble with such signs and attributions is that they exist within a collage of unresolved impressions, a pastiche of overlapping memories, literary influences, skimmings from the new psychologies of Freud and Havelock Ellis. When applied this way to the author's life, moreover, they violate the biographical facts. It was Leslie Stephen, for instance, who died a protracted death from cancer, and who stood as an impediment to Virginia's future life. Operated on in December 1902, given six months to live in the following May, he held on grimly until late in February 1904, as if unwilling to die. Meanwhile friends and relatives overwhelmed the family with farewell visits and outpouring sympathies, until Virginia rebelled against having her own emotions pumped out daily and caused a family row. There was good reason, then, to long for Stephen's death, and good reason, too, to see him as an impediment to future life, for as a widower his demands upon his daughters for support and sympathy (as upon his wife before them) had been unbearable. Whereas Julia Stephen had died from influenza within a period of eight weeks, and was a constant source of support and sympathy for her children (and above all for her husband) while she lived. Finally, our Freudian critic to the contrary notwithstanding, the oedipal Delia is based not upon Virginia but upon her older and bolder sister Vanessa, who did respond joyfully to her father's (not her mother's) death, whereas Virginia was painfully ambivalent and at times even excessive in her grief.[10]

Quite obviously, then, Virginia Woolf has imposed her father's prolonged death upon her mother in *The Years*, and has blended her unfeeling response to the first death with her sister's relief (in which she shared) at the second, as if compounding the two occasions into a catchall version of Victorian funereal gloom! The critic who can make biographical (not to say literary) sense out of this amalgam must be bold indeed. Then too, the Joycean parallels for admiring Parnell and scorning a dying mother must give us pause, as must the debunking work of Lytton Strachey where Colonel Pargiter's mistress is concerned. There is no evidence that Leslie Stephen ever had a mistress—though he did meet a friend of the Thackeray sisters, Julia Duckworth, on the eve of the night when his first wife, Minny Thackeray Stephen, expired from a sudden and wholly unexpected convulsion![11] One is tempted to conclude that Virginia Woolf is merely saying of such behavior, as of Delia's anger at her dying mother, Well, those cozy domestic Victorians were really like that; and being like that, apparently they produced lifelong bachelors and spinsters, homosexuals and lesbians, unsuitable marriages and bewildered children, with which the book is liberally sprinkled.

There is, all the same, one portion of the opening section of the novel which, properly sifted, may yield some useful biographical clues. On the eve of Rose Pargiter's death, her youngest daughter, who is also named Rose but who nonetheless models herself on her military father, asks her oldest sister Eleanor if she may go to the corner store, Lamley's, so as to buy the box of ducks in the window (as the Holograph version of the novel indicates, they are rubber ducks and she wants to float them in her tub).[12] Eleanor tells her she may go if her brother Martin will accompany her, but she mustn't go alone. At odds with brother Martin, who refuses to escort her, the adventurous Rose decides to go alone, steals her nurse's latchkey, and by seeing herself as Pargiter of Pargiter's horse riding on a desperate mission, she makes it to the store past the leering and presumably drunken man at the pillar-box who puts out an arm to stop her. On the way back, however, she sees the man under the gas lamp exposing himself to her and flees home with footsteps padding behind her. When Eleanor finds her awake that night, frightened and unable to sleep she is unable to tell her what has happened and says instead that she has had a bad dream. But Eleanor, sensing something more at stake, pushes for a better answer:

> "What was your dream about?" she asked, sitting down on the edge of the bed. Rose stared at her; she could not tell her; but at all costs Eleanor must be made to stay with her.
> "I thought I heard a man in the room," she brought out at last. "A robber," she added.
> "A robber? Here?" said Eleanor, "But Rose, how could a robber get into your nursery? There's Papa, there's Morris—they would never let a robber come into your room."
> "No," said Rose. "Papa would kill him" she added. There was something queer about the way she twitched. [*TY*, pp. 33–34]

Still unsatisfied, Eleanor asks again what has frightened her: " 'I saw . . . ' Rose began. She made a great effort to tell her the truth; to tell her about the man at the pillar-box. ' I saw . . . 'she repeated. But here the door opened and Nurse came in." (*TY*, p. 34) Late in her spinster life Rose is still unable to tell her interrupted story, though she vaguely feels the need to share it. More fortunate, Mrs. Woolf was able to tell portions of her own childhood experiences, in which, as we shall see, the robber—the man in the room—will acquire ghostly importance on the night after her mother's death, while the man at the pillar-box will prove to be —not merely the exhibitionist at Hyde Park Gate whom Virginia and Vanessa actually saw as children[13]—but a combination as well of the "idiot boy" (as Virginia benightedly calls him) who sprang up at her in Kensington Gardens in her childhood and her half brother Gerald Duckworth, who in a sense "exposed" her rather than himself when she was six. Meanwhile we have this interesting fictive connection between a dying mother, an older daughter's anger, and a child's first sexual fears.

"It is strange," says the grieving novelist Bernard in *The Waves*, "how the dead leap out on us at street corners, or in dreams" (*TW*, p. 274). The image anticipates Rose's experience with the leering man at the pillar-box, as does an earlier image of the randomness of death: "for there is neither rhyme nor reason when a drunk man staggers about with a club in his hand" (*TW*, p. 266). A man who walks "bang into the pillar-box" himself (*TW*, p. 292), Bernard sees death as the enemy as that novel ends, and like Rose Pargiter of Pargiter's horse, he has his desperate mission: "It is death against whom I ride with my spear couched and my hair flying back like a young man's, like Percival's, when he galloped in India. I strike spurs into my horse. Against you I will fling myself, unvanquished and unyielding, O Death!" (*TW*, p. 297).

Young Percival, based like Jacob Flanders on Virginia Woolf's dead brother Thoby, had been killed in India when his galloping horse stumbled and he was thrown to the ground. The central presence in this novel of six parentless peers whom he unifies, and who comprise between them one whole person, Percival-Thoby seems to have replaced Julia Stephen as the last complete person in modern times, and therefore as the prime antagonist-victim of senseless death. That he reappears at street corners or in dreams, and is victimized by a drunken man with a club, suggests the close (and decidedly ambivalent) correlation in the author's mind between the threat of sexual violation and the threat of death. The correlation is a familiar one in Woolf criticism; but its origins and consequences for her work have been imperfectly understood. With the recent appearance of her unpublished autobiographical writings, *Moments of Being* (1976), however, we can speculate on her obsessions with greater confi-dence.

The collection opens with her first and last memoirs, "Reminiscences" and "A Sketch of the Past," both of which cover those crucial early years when first her mother, then her half sister Stella Duckworth, then her sister Vanessa held the Stephen-Duckworth ménage together. The first memoir, written in 1907–08 when Virginia was in her mid-twenties, is the shorter and less rewarding work; but it dovetails with the richer "Sketch of the Past" in important ways. Here, for instance, we have the first written impression of Julia Stephen's first husband, Herbert Duckworth, the young barrister by whom she had borne three children, and with whom she was "happy as few people are happy" (*MB*, p. 32) in the brief years of their marriage. Woolf presents her mother's view of this husband much as Thackeray presents Amelia Sedley's cherished memories of her "saintly" husband George. Thus Julia had "cast over the figure of her bridegroom all the golden enchantments of Tennysonian senti-ment" (*MB*, p. 32); the years with him she had consecrated as "the golden ones," when "she had not known the sorrow and crime of the world because she had lived with a man, stainless of his kind, exalted in a world of pure love and beauty" (*MB*, p. 32). Over-whelmed by his death, she had abandoned her faith and her natural instinct for happiness, had in fact become an agnostic, and had spent the next eight years visiting the poor, nursing the sick and dying, confident that she possessed "the true secret of life at last . . . that sorrow is our lot, and at best we can but face it bravely" (*MB*, p. 32). With her second marriage her instinct for happiness revived, but it was the disillusioning stamp of lost love which would impress itself upon her children's memories. For them she appeared as a woman living "at high pressure" who invested all she did "with an inimitable bravery, as though she saw [life] properly composed, of fools and clowns and splendid Queens, a vast procession on the march towards death" (*MB*, pp. 35–36). She could be intensely preoccupied with events of the moment because of her "deep sense of the futility of all effort"; she could help others and make the most of what she had because of her "solemn doubt" about the future. This gave a melancholy "grandeur" to even her most trivial activities (*MB*, p. 36).

Her second husband's loss of his first wife through sudden death, his disturbed and backward child Laura by this marriage (perhaps by inheritance from the Thackeray line but perhaps also from the Stephen line), and his own stern agnostic philosophy, reinforced her attitudes, made him more attractive to her, and became the basis for their oddly morbid union. It was into this dubious household that Virginia Stephen was born in 1882, the third of four new offspring. There were eight children in all—four half brothers and four half sisters—from three different sets of parents. That Julia Stephen welded this ménage into a happy family over her last seventeen years is, needless to say, a tribute to her courage and resourcefulness; but she also exposed them to an undercurrent of romantic melancholy and a latent expectation of sudden loss. The legend of her first husband, as underscored by her grave moments and private sorrows, impressed at least one of her children all too deeply.

Thus, if she never spoke to them of her dead husband, the intensity of her happiness while he lived and her unhappiness when he died became family bywords. Virginia Woolf would write of that marriage seventy years after its tragic close as "the most important thing that ever happened to her" mother (MB, p. 89); she would repeat her mother's saying, as remembered by an older friend (Kitty Maxse), that Duckworth's death had made her "as unhappy as it is possible for a human being to be" (MB, p. 89); she would take her "complete collapse" at this time as proof of "how completely he satisfied her" and would cite her half sister Stella's story of how her mother "used to lie upon his grave at Orchardleigh" as proof of her "superlative" grief (MB, p. 90); and she would tell also the legend of Duckworth's sudden senseless death: how "he stretched to pick a fig for my mother; an abscess burst; and he died in a few hours" (MB, p. 89). If in her memoirs, early and late, she exhibits Thackerayan skepticism of her mother's view of barrister Duckworth as "the perfect man; heroic; handsome; magnanimous" (MB, pp. 89–90), she also indicates his romantic aura for all the children, and at one point, while trying to recall her mother's qualities, she even recalls her own romantic fantasy about him:

But apart from her beauty . . . what was she herself like? Very quick; very direct; practical; and amusing, I say at once offhand. She could be sharp, she disliked affectation. "If you put your head to one side like that, you shan't come to the party," I remember she said to me as we drew up in a carriage in front of some house. Severe; with a background of knowledge that made her sad. She had her own sorrow waiting behind her to dip into privately. *Once when she had set us to write exercises I looked up from mine and watched her reading–the Bible perhaps; and struck by the gravity of her face, told myself that her first husband had been a clergyman and that she was thinking, as she read what he had read, of him. That was a fable on my part; but it shows that she looked very sad when she was not talking.* [MB, p. 82; italics mine]

The sequence of thoughts here—her mother's sharpness and severity, her reprimand, her sorrow, then the fable of the clergyman lover whose loss still saddens her—yields important clues to the identity of the ghostly robber who appeared to Virginia on the night after her mother's death, and to her own inability to grieve that death. But to substantiate these clues we must focus still more intently on the rich series of associations and memories in the late memoir through which she finally reconstructs the sources of her lifelong distress.

"A Sketch of the Past" opens with Virginia's first memories, pleasant and unpleasant. The pleasant ones are of being on a train or bus with her mother, going (she prefers now to think) to St. Ives in Cornwall, where the Stephen-Duckworth ménage spent idyllic summers; and of lying half-asleep, half-awake, in her nursery bed at St. Ives, hearing the waves splashing on the beach outside and the yellow blind dragging its acorn across the floor as the wind blows, and feeling "the purest ecstasy" (MB, pp. 64–65). These intense impressions she now likens to "the feeling . . . of lying in a grape and seeing through a film of semi-transparent yellow" (MB, p. 65). They are womblike impressions, then, as of close maternal security, which may help to explain why she fixes her mind now on the nursery balcony, which joins the balcony of her parents' bedroom, as her mother emerges in a white dressing gown among the passion flowers; or why she moves to a later memory of beach-road gardens whose ripe sunny humming seems "to press voluptuously against some membrane" (*MB*, p. 66); or why she describes herself at such times as not a self, but "only the container of the feeling of ecstasy, of the feeling of rapture"—which accounts, she believes, for the strength "of all childhood memories" (*MB*, p. 66).

The unpleasant memory involves what she calls her "looking-glass shame" which began when she was six or seven and lasted all her life (*MB*, pp. 67–68). She had got into the habit of making sure she was alone, then standing tiptoe to see her face in the small mirror in the hall at St. Ives, and feeling ashamed of it. "A strong feeling of guilt seemed naturally attached to it," she adds (*MB*, p. 68), then tries to explain her reaction as going against her tomboy code about vanity, or as going with some inherited puritan instinct from her Clapham forebears. But the fact that she can also feel raptures disconnected with her body gives her pause: "I must have been ashamed or afraid of my own body," she concludes (*MB*, p. 68), and then cites another memory of the hall which "may help to explain this":

> There was a slab outside the dining room door for standing dishes upon. Once when I was very small Gerald Duckworth lifted me onto this, and as I sat there he began to explore my body. I can remember the feel of his hand going under my clothes; going firmly and steadily lower and lower. I remember how I hoped that he would stop; how I stiffened and wriggled as his hand approached my private parts. But it did not stop. His hand explored my private parts too. I remember resenting, disliking it—what is the word for so dumb and mixed a feeling? It must have been strong, since I still recall it. This seems to show that a feeling about certain parts of the body; how they must not be touched; how it is wrong to allow them to be touched; must be instinctive. It proves that Virginia Stephen was not born on the 25th January 1882, but was born many thousands of years ago; and had from the very first to encounter instincts already acquired by thousands of ancestresses in the past. [*MB*, p. 69]

Instinctive is certainly the right word for resistance to such violations, whether in childhood or adulthood; but the prohibi-

tions she invokes—"must not be touched," "wrong to allow them
to be touched"—were surely reinforced in early childhood by
concerned adults; and Woolf herself, dissatisfied by her ancestral
digression from the "looking-glass shame," now adds a dream
which "may refer to it";

> I dreamt that I was looking in a glass when a horrible face—the face
> of an animal—suddenly showed over my shoulder. I cannot be sure
> if this was a dream, or if it happened. Was I looking in the glass one
> day when something in the background moved, and seemed to me
> alive? I cannot be sure. But I have always remembered the other
> face in the glass, whether it was a dream or a fact, and that it
> frightened me. [*MB*, p. 69]

Whether this dreamed or hallucinated face is that of Gerald
Duckworth's animality, or her own, is probably irrelevant: let us
call it simply the frightening face of animal defilement, bestial
violation, of which she is both ashamed and guilty, as raped
women are seen to be guilty, even now, of their own violation. In
the same vein, the "mixed" feeling which she cannot name we
may attribute not to any physical sensation she may have felt,
though she does say she is "afraid" of her own body, but rather to
the fact that Gerald, at eighteen, an older and trusted half brother,
was using her in a way so shameful she could hardly speak of it.[14]
She does not tell us, for instance, that the incident was never
conveyed to her parents, nor to anyone else until this late memoir;
she does not consciously associate it with what might almost be
called the compensatory publication of her first two novels, in
1915 and 1919, by the same Gerald Duckworth, nor with the
anxieties and illnesses which followed all such publications. She
dredges it up now, rather, because she is heading for the sealing of
her unearned guilt which her mother's death assured.

Two more unpleasant memories seem relevant at this point:
during a fistfight with her brother Thoby, and upon hearing of a
neighbor's suicide, she is horrified to discover, first, that people
hurt each other and, second, that they may kill themselves; in both
cases she is held powerless and despairing, in a state of physical
collapse, by that "sense of horror" (*MB*, p. 71). Then, as the

memoir continues some two weeks later, she writes of two more "moments of being," from her walks in Kensington Gardens as a child, which bear upon such problems:

> There was the moment of the puddle in the path; when for no reason I could discover, everything suddenly became unreal; I was suspended; I could not step across the puddle; I tried to touch something . . . the whole world became unreal. Next, the other moment when the idiot boy sprang up with his hand outstretched mewing, slit-eyed, red-rimmed; and without saying a word, with a sense of the horror in me, I poured into his hand a bag of Russian toffee. But it was not over, for that night in the bath the dumb horror came over me. Again I had that hopeless sadness; that collapse I have described before; as if I were passive under some sledge-hammer blow; exposed to a whole avalanche of meaning that had heaped itself up and discharged itself upon me, unprotected, with nothing to ward it off, so that I huddled up at my end of the bath, motionless. I could not explain it; I said nothing even to Nessa sponging herself at the other end. [MB, p. 78]

These are her first unpleasant memories of water. Her unreal and almost schizoid suspension at the puddle seems too vague to fathom—was it a ground mirror into which she might disappear? was it a pool she might drown in (as when she speaks of the decision reached with Leonard to commit suicide if the Germans invaded England in 1940 as "that dismal puddle" [MB, p. 100])? or does its connection with the next memory confirm some sexual fear? Certainly her dumb horror in the bath reminds us of Rose Pargiter's quest for bathtub toys in The Years, and of her inability to tell her older sister what had happened at the pillar-box. The "mewing" boy with hand outstretched reminds us too of the leering man who reached out for Rose as she passed, and who even "made a mewing noise" (TY, p. 24), sucking his lips in and out while his hands unbuttoned his clothes, on her precarious return. Then too, Virginia's odd response to the "mewing" boy—her gift of toffee as if to ward off or propitiate that outstretched hand — has decided connections with Gerald Duckworth's exploring hand in what seems to be the earlier episode. As their fictional fusion suggests, these episodes carry a heavy overload of psychic meaning: the threatening boy and the threatening half brother; the threatening madness of her "idiot" half sister Laura; her powerless, passive collapse before sledge-hammer blows which her mother faces bravely, and with such melancholy grandeur. There are enough overwhelming feelings here already to account, in some part, for Virginia's response to the sledge-hammer blow of her mother's death.

The expanded account of that death in 1939 differs in several respects from the brief descriptions of 1924 and 1934. First of all, there were two visits to her mother's deathbed, one early in the morning of May 5, 1895, the other the next evening. Second, it was her older half brother George Duckworth, and not his sister Stella, who took the children in when Virginia felt the "desire to laugh"; Stella would take her in alone on the second visit. In 1934 Woolf's memory had selected the least painful aspects of both occasions, choosing Stella over George because his behavior in ensuing years had given her ample cause to repress him, and leaving the actual visit with Stella untouched because it was, in fact, horrendous. But let us take each visit as it comes. The first is described in two segments, one at the end of the long May 2d entry (written only three days from the forty-fourth anniversary of her mother's death), the other at the beginning of the next entry, nearly four weeks later:

> George took us down to say goodbye. My father staggered from the bedroom as we came. I stretched out my arms to stop him, but he brushed past me, crying out something I could not catch; distraught. And George led me in to kiss my mother, who had just died.

> May 28th 1939. Led by George with towels wrapped round us and given each a drop of brandy in warm milk to drink, we were taken into the bedroom. I think candles were burning; and I think the sun was coming in. At any rate I remember the long looking-glass; with the drawers on either side; and the washstand; and the great bed on which my mother lay. I remember very clearly how even as I was taken to the bedside I noticed that one nurse was sobbing, and a desire to laugh came over me, and I said to myself as I have often done at moments of crisis since, "I feel nothing what-

ever". Then I stooped and kissed my mother's face. It was still warm. She had only died a moment before. Then we went upstairs into the day nursery. [*MB*, pp. 91–92]

In this more fully remembered version of the first visit it is Virginia who stretches out her arms to stop a passing figure. But, unlike Delia in *The Years*, she has no doubts about her father's grief; he is not pretending but is, quite simply, "distraught." If she wants to halt him, to comfort and be comforted, their common need for reassurance has to be weighed against any "childish sense of rivalry" with her mother we might posit here; and, as we shall see, that need may have a quite different meaning for her, of common loss rather than common gain. Once more, as in 1934 (though not in 1924), it is the nurse who touches off the desire to laugh, but the defensive need to accuse her of pretending has given way to an even greater sense of insufficient feeling. The stress now is on *feeling nothing whatever*, and that indicates, I think, a state of numbness sealed rather than caused by the father's rejection of her proffered arms. The long looking glass—even the towels and washstand—may help us here. They seem innocent enough, as itemized among other and less well-remembered aspects of the scene; but Woolf's recollection of her looking-glass shame in previous pages, and of her dumb bathtub horrors, makes them stand out now as reminders of fear and defilement. Consider too Rose Pargiter's quest for bathtub toys, and such stories as "An Unwritten Novel" (1920), in which a melancholy woman—one who avoids looking glasses—has committed the "crime" of shopping late for her own pleasure (like Rose Pargiter) while her mother dies; and "The Lady in the Looking-Glass" (1929), which begins and ends with the statement: "People should not leave looking-glasses hanging in their rooms any more than they should leave open cheque books or letters confessing some hideous crime."[15] We have license, then, to take such objects seriously as signs of guilt and shame. We know, further, that children often feel that divorcing parents leave them because they have done something wrong; and that they also feel angry about being left: so too with dying parents. These are points to keep in mind, at any rate, as we look at the second and surely the more disastrous visit:

Perhaps it was the next evening that Stella took me into the bedroom to kiss mother for the last time. She had been lying on her side before. Now she was lying straight in the middle of her pillows. Her face looked immeasurably distant, hollow and stern. When I kissed her, it was like kissing cold iron. Whenever I touch cold iron the feeling comes back to me—the feeling of my mother's face, iron cold, and granulated. I started back. Then Stella stroked her cheek, and undid a button on her nightgown. "She always liked to have it like that," she said. When she came up to the nursery later she said to me, "Forgive me. I saw you were afraid." She had noticed that I had started. When Stella asked me to forgive her for having given me that shock, I cried—we had been crying off and on all day—and said, "When I see mother, I see a man sitting with her." Stella looked at me as if I had frightened her. Did I say that in order to attract attention to myself? Or was it true? I cannot be sure, for certainly I had a great wish to draw attention to myself. *But certainly it was true that when she said: "Forgive me," and thus made me visualize my mother, I seemed to see a man sitting bent on the edge of the bed.*

"It's nice that she shouldn't be alone", Stella said after a moment's pause. [*MB*, p. 92; italics mine]

Virginia Woolf goes on to say that "any hallucination was possible" in the "melodramatic, histrionic and unreal" atmosphere of "those three or four days before the funeral"; and she cites the hushed, closed rooms, the artificial light, the hall reeking of flowers, the people creeping in and out. But we have good reason to believe that this particular hallucination was waiting for some time to surface, and that it explains more than any other factor her odd desire to laugh, her inability to feel grief in her mother's presence. If the man on the edge of the bed is the clergyman lover, Herbert Duckworth, of Virginia's earlier fantasy; if the absolving words, "Forgive me," are magic words which she wants to hear from her mother, and which now enable her to grieve for her and to visualize her together with her first and long-dead husband; and if that iron-cold feeling confirms her fear that her mother's warmth is being denied her in the interest of just such a deathly reunion—a return, as it were, to eternal happiness along the idyllic lines of her first marriage; then Herbert Duckworth is the robber, the man whom Rose Pargiter sees in her room in *The Years*, and whom Papa would indeed kill if he were not (as it were) already dead. Herbert Duckworth is the thief of love; he has stolen back his rightful bride; and Virginia, who wants and needs attention now, is very angry that her mother has left her to rejoin this handsome, heroic, bible-reading thief who will twelve years later seem "so obviously her inferior in all ways" (*MB*, p. 32). (No need to cry about *that* departure! But much need to laugh when others do.) She has good psychic reason, then, as a child, to want to embrace her distraught father, who has also lost out to this handsome ghostly robber; and even better reason to be angry with her agnostic mother for creating such a religious escape hatch for herself, if only in Virginia's hallucinating mind.

For Duckworth has long been waiting there for his beloved Julia. While she lived he was the sorrow waiting behind her into which she privately dipped, as Virginia would later dip for her lost dead; but now, supplanting her own father, he is the eternally perfect lover to whom her mother has returned—though paradoxically, in the persons of his sons, first Gerald and later George, he is also earthly defilement for Virginia, if not for *her* beloved Julia—and who will now explain such baffling differences to her? Not Stella Duckworth, who now compounds them by undoing a button on her mother's nightgown—though at least she seems to catch the allusion to her own father when it comes, and with remarkable kindness and not a little prescience, she makes his ghostly reunion with their common mother seem companionable, and therefore humanly comforting, and so defuses for a time the secret cause of resentful laughter of the previous morning. But that immeasurably distant face, that iron-cold rejection, that perfect and now eternal happiness, that strong sense of unworthiness, that total sense of loss, and above all that appalling anger in a child who would rather be powerless than hurt her mother, have begun their life's work. That summer Virginia would begin to hear voices, would collapse completely as her mother had collapsed before her at her first husband's death, and would list among her physical and emotional symptoms her intolerable depressions and her terror and shame at meeting other people.[16]

3 Funereal Gloom

The house at Abercorn Terrace was very dark. It smelt strongly of spring flowers. For some days now wreaths had been piled one on top of another on the hall table. In the dimness—all the blinds were drawn—the flowers gleamed; and the hall smelt with the amorous intensity of a hothouse. Wreath after wreath, they kept arriving. . . .

Even now with the hearse at the door the bell rang; a messenger boy appeared bearing more lilies. He raised his cap, as he stood in the hall, for men were lurching down the stairs carrying the coffin. . . . The family followed after. . . .

At last they reached the cemetery. As she took her place in the little group behind the coffin and walked up to the church, [Delia] was relieved to find that she was overcome by some generalized and solemn emotion. . . . Then the service began. A clergyman, a cousin, read it. . . .

"I am the resurrection and the life."

Pent up as she had been all these days in the half-lit house which smelt of flowers, the outspoken words filled her with glory. This she could feel genuinely; this was something that she said herself. But then, as Cousin James went on reading, something slipped. The sense was blurred. She could not follow with her reason. . . . Then Cousin James seemed to hurry, as if he did not altogether believe what he was saying. He seemed to pass from the known to the unknown; from what he believed to what he did not believe; even his voice altered. . . . She gave it up. Either one understood or one did not understand, she thought. Her mind wandered.

The Years (pp. 65–67)

In "Reminiscences" Virginia Woolf had spoken of her mother's death as "the greatest disaster that could happen" and had described the "period of Oriental gloom" which followed as one "that passed the normal limits of sorrow" (*MB*, p. 40). In "A Sketch of the Past" she described her feeling that "everything had come to an end" (*MB*, p. 84): "With mother's death the merry, various life which she had held in being shut for ever" (*MB*, p. 93). Certainly the impact of her death, the loss of the very center and creator of the family's common happy life, was profound enough to effect an almost total change. But perhaps "Victorian" is a better word than "Oriental" for the excessive and abnormal gloom which accompanied that change: for the sense of unnaturalness which came to the Stephen children was a sign of their modernity, of their need to break with elaborate forms of mourning which may have given comfort in an age of waning faith and many deaths, but which no longer ministered to emotional needs. Both Julia and Leslie Stephen were pronounced agnostics who had renounced comforting faiths; they may have found some compensation in the Victorian tradition of extended and belabored mourning. But their children had no comforting faiths to lose—only disturbing hallucinations or, at best, latent religious yearnings; they needed emotional redirection toward "life itself" rather than immersion in needless formal gloom.

Then too, the nature of the bond between Julia and Leslie Stephen was painfully Victorian at a time when new possibilities in married relations were beginning to emerge. In his incessant demands for support and sympathy from his wife, Stephen was more like an older child with paternal privileges than a husband and lover; and in this he was typical of his age.[1] Similarly Julia's support was typically maternal; her self-sacrifice to her husband (as to her children) was made at the expense of her health and personal welfare, and without question it led to her early death at forty-nine—another Victorian "tradition." If there was love and respect between these two, it was uxorious rather than passionately romantic love like that which Julia had known, or thought she had known, with fig-picking Herbert Duckworth. The distinction is important because, traditional or not, Leslie Stephen's mode of grieving was excessive; it reflected his essential *dependency* upon his wife for emotional support, not his strength as a loving equal. His demands for support and sympathy in his grief from Julia's daughters were like those made upon Julia while she lived; but his children had no wifely warrant for supplying them in such abundance, or for reinforcing them with either passional or maternal warmth.

Stella Duckworth, who replaced her mother as mistress of the large mourning household, was the first daughter to confront Stephen's demands. It was Stella who kept him occupied, got him to talk when he sat sunk in gloom, soothed and absolved him when he paced up and down, raving wildly that he had never told Julia how he loved her (*MB*, p. 94). In "A Sketch of the Past" Virginia describes Stella, interestingly, as having been raised in the shade of her mother's widowhood; she "saw that beautiful crape-veiled figure daily; and perhaps took then the ply that was so marked—that attitude of devotion, almost canine in its touching adoration, to her mother; that passive, suffering affection; and also that complete unquestioning dependence" (*MB*, p. 96). Her mother had treated her as her selfless handmaid, in those years of mourning, and Leslie Stephen came to expect the same selfless service to his grief. As Virginia puts it in "Reminiscences": "he expected entire self-surrender on her part; and had decided apparently, and with sufficient reason, that she possessed one of those beautiful natures which are quite without wishes of their own" (*MB*, p. 48). To Virginia and Vanessa, who would soon experience it for themselves, this extreme form of Victorian devotion was so patently demeaning as to push them toward the opposite extreme when freedom came.

For Stella the chance for freedom came in the person of her once-rejected suitor, Jack Hills. A solicitor and country gentleman, Hills had been one of her mother's favorite young men; thanks to her patient negotiations, he had returned to press his case, as it happened, on the night of Julia's death—and it may be that Virginia fused him in her mind, as time went on, with her mother's ghostly companion. Stella continued to see him with growing appreciation of his steady qualities, and about a year and a quarter later they became engaged (as it were) with her mother's dying sanction. By contrast, Leslie Stephen took the engagement as an irreparable blow; he considered Stella indispensable to himself, and exacted from her the promise that she and Jack would come to live with the family when they married—then exploded when they wisely decided to break that promise. For Virginia, however, the engagement was like the rebirth of that romantic love she had glimpsed in the legend of Herbert Duckworth. As she writes in her late memoir: "it was through that engagement that I had my first vision—so intense, so exciting, so rapturous was it that the word vision applies—my first vision then of love between man and woman.... It gave me a conception of love; a standard of love; a sense that nothing in the whole world is so lyrical, so musical, as a young man and a young woman in their first love for each other" (MB, p. 105). Then she adds, rather sharply, that she connects such love with "respectable engagements" and that "unofficial loves" or "affairs" never give her the same feeling. The distinction was no doubt reinforced by Jack Hills's open, whole-some, humorous, and deliberate attempt, as Virginia oddly saw it, to educate her on "the part played by sex in the life of the ordinary man," for whom "having women was a mere trifle" (MB, p. 104).

The prospect of the coming marriage was anything but trifling. There would be a house untouched by gloom to which the children could retreat; there would be a chance for a similar inde-pendent life for the young half sisters; and Stella, like her mother before her with Jack Hills, would negotiate for them in the dif-ficult business of achieving it. As she told one of their aunts, "she was to float us on the life of love; to launch us out on the ordinary woman's life that promised such treasures" (MB, p. 106). And she was in fact able to witness Vanessa's "coming out" in a brief respite from the illness which led to her death, and to feel then "what a mother would have felt" and "the sort of triumph" that she herself had just attempted (MB, p. 53). But on July 27, 1897, three months after her marriage to Jack Hills, she died of compli-cations attending pregnancy and appendicitis; and on June 8, 1940, almost forty-three years later, Virginia could still reflect bitterly on "how different 'coming out' and those Greek slave years and all their drudgery and tyranny and rebellion would have been," had Stella lived (MB, p. 106).

The "Greek slave years" were those which followed when Virginia and Vanessa had to cope alone with Leslie Stephen's growing tyranny. Meanwhile the nightmare of their mother's death had been repeated and another period of funereal gloom had ensued: "Once again we went through the same expressions of sympathy; we heard again and again that so great a tragedy had never happened; sometimes it appeared almost in the light of a work of art; more often it revealed a shapeless catastrophe, from which there could be no recovery" (*MB*, p. 55). The lines are instructive in that Virginia Woolf would herself use art to cope with such catastrophes; but it is the artifice of mourning which offends her now. In "Reminiscences" she would speak of the pain of her mother's death as at least being real in comparison with the "sultry and opaque" life which followed, the tears, groans, and self-reproaches of her father and his friends, which converted Julia from a true and vivid woman into "an unlovable phantom" (*MB*, p. 45); and again in "A Sketch of the Past" she would prefer unhappiness to the travesties of Victorian mourning:

> The tragedy of her death was not that it made one, now and then and very intensely, unhappy. It was that it made her unreal, and us solemn, and self-conscious. We were made to act parts that we did not feel; to fumble for words that we did not know. It obscured, it dulled. It made one hypocritical and inmeshed in the conventions of sorrow. Many foolish and sentimental ideas came into being. Yet there was a struggle . . . a conflict between what we ought to be and what we were. Thoby put this into words. One day before he went back to school, he said: "It's silly going on like this . . . ", sobbing, sitting shrouded, he meant. I was shocked by his heartlessness; yet he was right, I know. [*MB*, p. 95]

Compare her own "heartlessness" at her mother's deathbed—her secret laughter, her feeling "nothing whatever," her fearful hallucination—reinforced now by the need to break with excessive grieving and its conventional forms—and compounded twice over by the grievings and conventions, two years later, which came with Stella's death. Her delight then in leaving behind "the ghastly mourners" when the family took a summer home (*MB*, p. 55) would turn to active rebellion, seven years later, when she could no longer put up with the demands of relatives to share in their emotions during her father's prolonged dying. By then she was a confirmed modern sensibility in her repulsion from Victorian funereal gloom; and for many years to come the "conflict between what we ought to be and what we were" would cover up her need to work through the grief, guilt, and anger of these deaths.

The tragic end of the romance of Jack and Stella was equally disastrous in its reinforcements. Her confusion over her mother's first romantic marriage and her own defilement was compounded now by new developments. Observing that Leslie Stephen was untouched by Stella's death, and "was quite prepared to take Vanessa as his next victim" (*MB*, p. 56), both Vanessa and Virginia turned instinctively to comfort the better mourner, Jack Hills, who at least understood their misery. Their readiness to comfort the young mourner, and their previous difficulties in comforting their father, was partly a matter of age, as Virginia saw in retrospect, for Stephen was sixty-five when his second wife died and had little in common with his children. But there was much justice in their complaint that he was willing to enslave them for his own selfish needs, whereas Jack had insisted on Stella's worth and had tried to secure it. The difference in age took a romantic turn, however, as both sisters kept lonely vigils with the bereft husband and Vanessa gradually came to love him, and to replace Stella in his affections. Virginia's innocence of these developments at fifteen was mixed with subconscious awareness of Jack's sexual anguish and some jealousy of her older sister, as she later saw (*MB*, pp. 56, 121); but she rallied to Vanessa's side when her half brother George Duckworth asked her to interfere to prevent a public scandal (*MB*, p. 122), and the family was soon embroiled in one of those bitter quarrels which seemed endemic to their sorrow.

George Duckworth's concern with outward show would further compound the sexual confusion of these years. In the early and late memoirs Virginia Woolf would depict him as steeped in the Victorian conventions, as socially successful, especially with women, and as a puzzling mixture of heroic devotion to his motherless sisters, whom he proposed to introduce to society, and of selfish pursuit of his own social ambitions; and she would hint also at the brutishness under "the purity of his love" and at the odd intensity of his brotherly affections. In a separate memoir of 1920, written for a group of Bloomsbury sophisticates, she would develop these hints into a satire of George as a brainless Victorian snob with the curls of a god, the ears of a faun, and the eyes of a pig (*MB*, p. 144). As a god he taught games to his small half brothers and half sisters, read aloud to them when they were ill, took them to the pantomime, remembered the birthdays of aunts, sent turtle soup to invalids, and braved their father's ire. As a faun he was sportive and demonstrative. Tears flowed profusely from his eyes as from a font of deep, warm feeling (*MB*, p. 145). Kisses came from his mouth with equal ease, as when he refused to argue with those he loved and would drown them instead in kisses (*MB*, p. 147). But gradually his piggishness emerged as it became evident that he was using his half sisters to advance himself socially, and not simply lavishing his affection upon them but seducing them as well, as when he pursued them at night into their darkened bedrooms (*MB*, p. 155). As I have elsewhere argued, the recent dispute as to whether Virginia imagined (hence desired) such erotic attentions seems to me ill-founded; her friend Janet Case had witnessed and had been repelled by George's nursery fondlings (*QB* 1:43n); her sister Vanessa seems to have reported them to Virginia's doctor (*QB* 1:96n); and as the memoir implies, Vanessa herself had suffered similar treatment from him (*MB*, pp. 149, 155). If Virginia embroiders her memorial accounts for aesthetic effect, as Jean Love argues, she deals nonetheless with a common Victorian problem—the erotic direction of intense family affections—and has witnesses for her case.[2]

It was George's histrionics, at any rate, as much as her father's, which prepared Virginia for the debunking of Victorian sentimentality as to love and marriage in the Bloomsbury years when she and Vanessa entertained a circle of their brothers' college friends. As we learn in "Old Bloomsbury," these Cambridge intellectuals talked abstractly and openly about adultery, copulation, and buggery and altogether ignored those "respectable engagements" she secretly admired (*MB*, pp. 169, 174). That most of these young men were homosexual did not especially trouble her; she had read about buggery in Plato, and was relieved in any case by the freedom from George's hypocritical affections (*MB*, p. 172). With these young men affectionate *asexual* relations were possible; there was no confusion of romance with defilement— indeed there was no romance. One could be companionable with these and other men; but romantic and passionate love was something she could feel, apparently, only for women,[3] partly because the taboo against consummation kept it pure, but chiefly because the women in her family—her mother, Stella Duckworth,

Vanessa—had been the only persons who had loved her unselfishly and unstintingly, with the possible exception of her undemonstrative brother Thoby.

The close companionship with Thoby, intensified by their common awareness of "the insecurity of life" (MB, p. 117), and the sporadic occasions when her father proved a delightful intellectual companion and supportive mentor, kept her from altogether despising men and made possible her companionate marriage with Leonard Woolf. But she had wanted and needed much more than this from her father. After her mother's death there had been, from time to time, an "odd fumbling fellowship" in common loss (MB, p. 117); and in his closing years, when the children were old enough for real companionship, he began to feel a special tenderness for Virginia and found her "most fascinating" (QB 1:87–88). But her strongest feelings during these years were rage and resentment. Her father had been "the tyrant of inconceivable selfishness, who had replaced the beauty and merriment of the dead with ugliness and gloom" (MB, p. 56). He had expected Vanessa to be "part slave, part angel of sympathy" (MB, p. 125), as Stella and Julia had been before her, and to cater as they had to his whims: "When he was sad, he explained, she should be sad; when he was angry, as he was periodically when she asked him for a cheque, she should weep" (MB, p. 56). His kitchen rages, at household accounting times, were incredibly savage; so much so that Virginia later theorized that "whole tracts of his sensibility" had been atrophied by the crippling effects of his one-sided education and intensive scholarship (MB, p. 126). Though he expressed his own feelings effusively, with histrionic groans and flourishes, "he had no idea what other people felt" and "did not realise what he did" to them (MB, p. 126). He did it, moreover, only to women, on whom he depended for that consolation for professional failure he was ashamed to seek from men (MB, p. 125). But he did it also from his grandfatherly stance in the Victorian past, from which position, given his Edwardian daughters' vision of the future, no communication was possible. It was, as Virginia later saw, a cultural standoff: "We were not his children, but his grandchildren. When we both felt that he was not only terrifying but also ridiculous we were looking at him with eyes that saw ahead of us something—something so easily seen now by every boy and girl of sixteen or eighteen that the sight is perfectly familiar" (*MB*, p. 126).

It seems evident from all this that Virginia wanted from her father an understanding of her feelings he could not give and a youthful heroism and strength he did not possess. She desperately needed a considerate and romantically appealing father whose love would free her—not so much from the Victorian past—but from its ghosts and defilements, its unrelieved griefs, its triflings and seductions, and above all, its enslavements. What she got was an aging, emotionally obtuse, irascible scholar who had no idea where she was, who she was, or what she needed, but who did show a special fondness for her in his closing years.

Her feelings at his death were inevitably ambivalent and unresolved. She had rebelled against grieving visitors in his final days; but after his death she became irritated with her brothers and her sister for not grieving at all. She found Vanessa's open relief and happiness at their newfound freedom intolerable; and yet she shared in the common merriment. At other times she grieved excessively and possessively, like her father before her. She believed that "she had never done enough for him," that "she had never told him how much she valued him," that a true relationship was just beginning when he died, that no one but herself could understand what he was like (*QB* 1:87–89). As such vacillations show, she wanted him to die and felt guilty about her immense relief; but she also wanted him to live because she desperately needed his real and potential love. She became feverish and morbid as she tried to cope with these confusions, she began to hear voices, and that summer went into her second major breakdown. Her excessive and ambivalent grief had only further compounded her secret laughter at her mother's deathbed, even as her half brother George Duckworth's bedroom attentions, while her father lay dying, had further compounded her secret shame.[4]

The four Stephen children set up a common household when Virginia mended. Free of trifling and effusive Duckworths, free of their father's glooms and rages, they seemed to be living at last in the Edwardian present. But two years later Thoby died of typhoid fever and Vanessa quickly married and moved out, as if to escape the family contagion. Virginia lived on with her younger brother Adrian. She had loved Thoby but had not known much about him. She would try to recreate him in two elegiac fictions, *Jacob's Room* and *The Waves*, but as I have said, he exists in both more as an absence than a presence, and so eludes her need to reclaim him. But at least he becomes the missing Percival, the missing gallant knight, in her mother's vast procession on the march toward death, "of fools and clowns and splendid Queens."

When Vanessa was about to marry Clive Bell, Henry James had visited the new Stephen household and, in recording his visit, had remarked on the presence of boisterous love "in that house of all the Deaths," and on "the hungry *futurity* of youth" when all he "could mainly see" were the ghosts of Thoby, Stella, Leslie, and Julia, "on all of whom these young backs were, quite naturally, so gaily turned."5 The list of ghosts was at least two short, if we may add the shades of Minny Thackeray and Herbert Duckworth; and the gayness was, in Virginia's case, deceptive. She was to take all these ghosts with her into her futurity, at some cost to her sanity, and to make healing fictions out of the tensions between surface gaiety and their unstilled claims. Her struggle to put these spirits to rest is one of the more heroic annals of modern fiction, and deserves to be recorded in some such terms.

In many ways, for example, she was engaged from childhood on in a conflict as devastating in its toll on feelings and relations as the First World War. She suffered personally from as many casualties in family ranks as did any combatant from the loss of comrades; and the disruptions in her family life were as great as those effected by the war. Her form of shell shock was domestic and familial, and it was produced by a series of deaths and shiftings of family fronts which reinforced many times over that "legacy of pessimism" her mother had bequeathed her (*QB* 2:256). One of its obvious consequences, moreover, was to erase whole ranges of Victorian sentiment from her sensibility, especially those involving mourning and (after *Night and Day*) romantic love; and such erasures, as we know from Hemingway and Wilfred Owen and others like them, were also among the demonstrable effects of World War I. In the pages which follow I want to examine these consequences in what I take to be her two finest and most important novels, *Mrs Dalloway* and *To the Lighthouse*.

4 Mrs. Dalloway's Absent Grief

Of Mrs. Dalloway then one can only bring to light at the moment a few scraps, of little importance or none perhaps; as that in the first version Septimus, who later is intended to be her double, had no existence; and that Mrs. Dalloway was originally to kill herself, or perhaps merely to die at the end of the party. Such scraps are offered humbly to the reader in the hope that like other odds and ends they may come in useful.

Introduction, Mrs. Dalloway[1]

Then Joyce is dead . . . and the books, I suppose, take their place in the long procession.

A Writer's Diary (p. 363)

As early as 1919, when in "Modern Fiction" she had defined life as "a luminous halo, a semi-transparent envelope surrounding us from the beginning of consciousness to the end" (CE 2:106), Virginia Woolf had indicated her attraction to Joyce's stream-of-consciousness method in *Ulysses* and to its solipsistic intensities. Her objection to his method—that it was "centred in a self which . . . never embraces or creates what is outside itself and beyond" (CE 2:l08)—had of course signaled her own intention to reach outward from the flow of consciousness to apprehend a less alien world. Her objection to the mind behind the method—its "comparative poverty," its deliberate indecencies—indicated also her intention to be more "jovial and magnanimous," and decidedly more discreet, in dealing with life's social and personal amenities (CE 2:108; 1:334–35). Privately she had referred less kindly to Joyce's "filth," a subject to which she would return with increasing vehemence as she read more deeply into the text;[2] and yet in 1919, on the basis of first impressions of the early chapters, it was Joyce's spirituality which attracted her. It separated him

from "materialists" like Arnold Bennett, and, in the "Hades"
chapter especially, it brought him closer to her own preoccupation. Thus she writes in "Modern Fiction":

> In contrast with those whom we have called materialists, Mr. Joyce
> is spiritual; he is concerned at all costs to reveal the flickerings of
> that innermost flame which flashes its messages through the brain,
> and in order to preserve it he disregards with complete courage
> whatever seems to him adventitious. . . . *The scene in the cemetery,*
> *for instance, with its brilliancy, its sordidity, its incoherence, its*
> *sudden flashes of significance, does undoubtedly come so close to*
> *the quick of the mind that, on a first reading at any rate, it is*
> *difficult not to acclaim a masterpiece. If we want life itself, here*
> *surely we have it.* [CW 2:107; italics mine]

Yes, life itself—but life, oddly, in the cemetery, where the
innermost consciousness is chiefly engaged in apprehending
death! It was this kind of spirituality, and the courage to preserve
it, which she admired in Joyce and wanted somehow to emulate.

By 1922, when she began writing *Mrs. Dalloway*, she had
finally read *Ulysses* in full and had begun to assimilate its subjective possibilities for her fiction.[3] In her previous novel, *Jacob's
Room* (1922), she had employed an experimental method closer
to Katherine Mansfield's than to Joyce's. What she offered, in
effect, was a brief life history of a young war-victim, Jacob Flanders, as conveyed by the random impressions of other characters,
and from time to time through his own impressions. Her method
was lyric, poetic, oblique; it afforded a great deal of tantalizing
mystery about Jacob's inner nature, and very little inner substance. Joyce's stream-of-consciousness method brought her
closer, however, to "the quick of the mind," or to her own
touchstone for reality, the "luminous halo" of "life itself," as she
began her new novel.

At first it was the expansive, selfless quality of the luminous
mind which intrigued her. As she wrote in her diary in 1920, the
danger for her kind of psychological fiction was "the damned
egotistical self"; it had ruined Joyce and Dorothy Richardson,
made them narrow and restricted. Unless she were "pliant and

rich enough to provide a wall for the book from [herself]" it might cramp her too (*WD*, p. 23). So in *Mrs. Dalloway* she devised a kind of common selfless consciousness as her pliant wall, an unobtrusive authorial voice which blended with the flowing thoughts of her characters and, on occasion, made them equally selfless.

The technical term for such a voice is *indirect interior monologue*, a form of reported inner speech by which the author speaks for the character's flowing thoughts. Joyce used it moderately in *Ulysses* to get inside his characters' minds, where—given his belief in the mind's resources—he wanted to stay as long as possible; for similar reasons, yet with much less substantiality, Dorothy Richardson used it as her controlling mode in *Pilgrimage*;[4] but Virginia Woolf went inside in *Mrs. Dalloway* so as to come back out. She wanted her characters to use her bridging voice to embrace and create the world; she wanted them to receive mystic messages, to achieve romantic oneness with urban flux or with natural surroundings, and to dissolve into such surroundings after death. Her version of the stream was accordingly more spiritual than Joyce's, more open and expansive, and also more accessible to "the common reader." The language of her common selfless voice was more uniformly conventional, for instance, than Joyce's varied, idiomatic, and sometimes fractured language; and for better or worse it extended to all her characters, who tend to speak and think in her own literary accents, in her own slightly Victorian diction. Thus, in "A Sketch of the Past," she would dwell on the disadvantages for her writing of having been trained in "the Victorian game of manners":

> We still play the game. It is useful; it has its beauty, for it is founded upon restraint, sympathy, unselfishness—all civilised qualities. It is helpful in making something seemly and human out of raw odds and ends. But the Victorian manner is perhaps—I am not sure—a disadvantage in writing. When I re-read my old *Common Reader* articles I detect it there. I lay the blame for their suavity, their politeness, their sidelong approach, to my tea-table training. I see myself handing plates of buns to shy young men and asking them, not directly and simply about their poems and their novels, but

whether they like cream as well as sugar. On the other hand, this surface manner allows one to say a great many things which would be inaudible if one marched straight up and spoke out. [*MB*, p. 129]

Of course, her critical and her fictive voices are not wholly identical; but "restraint, sympathy, unselfishness"—with those civilized qualities she could also avoid the "raw odds and ends," the "raw flesh" she abhorred in Joyce's fiction, and could give us, in *Mrs. Dalloway*, her own "cooked flesh" (*WD*, p. 47). Her Victorian "surface manner" would be even subtler in its audibilities, but it would also recall the tea-table delicacies of which Henry James was accused by admirers of more rough and ready accents[5]—as when the bells of St. Margaret's toll "like a hostess who comes into her drawing room on the very stroke of the hour and finds her guests there already," and, reluctant to impose her "individuality" upon them, disperses herself into their hearts like the confiding and restful Clarissa "coming down the stairs on the stroke of the hour in white"—until "the sudden loudness of the final strike" tolls for Clarissa's death (*MD*, pp. 74–75). All subtly and poignantly done, but the cost of such delicacy would be the kind of avoidances Virginia Woolf had belatedly detected in her criticism.

Consider her own raw motives for exploring death-directed apprehensions in this manner. The common selfless voice resembles in some measure her childhood feeling of "lying in a grape and seeing through a film of transparent yellow" (*MB*, p. 65). Her sense of being at such times not a self, but "only the container of the feeling of ecstasy, of the feeling of rapture" (*MB*, p. 66), inheres in her newfound narrative manner, and the securities of such regressive containment—the ecstasies and raptures—lead also in deathly directions, as James Naremore has so lucidly shown.[6] Clarissa's life-raptures, for instance, her dissolving fusions with flowers and city streets, are part of a transcendental theory whereby the "unseen part" of herself will survive after death, will be "laid out like a mist" among the people and places it has known (*MD*, pp. 12, 231–32); and the author supports her theory by her own selfless presence, by the apprehensions of other characters—Peter Walsh, Septimus Warren Smith, Maisie Johnson, Elizabeth Dalloway—and by that mystic communion between the dead Smith and the live Clarissa with which the novel ends, and by which Clarissa avoids her own suicide. Thus, if the author's selfless manner has distinct aesthetic advantages, if it enables outward reachings and embracings and makes thoughts and ideas accessible, it works also as a defensive strategy—like Clarissa's—for descending into Hades as anyone but her troubled self.

Fortunately there were other lessons to be learned from assimilating Joyce's method. The time scheme in *Ulysses*—marking out the hours of a single day in prewar Dublin so as to give external order to internal flux—would seem so "original" to Woolf that she thought she had invented the "design" herself and for a long time called her book *The Hours* (*WD*, p. 58); and yet, whatever their sources, the tolling bells in this novel help to suggest a pressing, shifting, and distinctly threatening world. The social scope of Joyce's urban novel, and its frequent satiric note, would also inspire her to want "to criticise the social system, and to show it at work, at its most intense"—but fearing she might be "posing" in this capacity, she wisely abandoned an early attempt at political satire for a broader and more telling version of urban alienation (*WD*, p. 57). Her most important discovery, however, was her "tunneling process," whereby she learned to tell the past by installments, as she needed it. It had taken a year's groping to learn for herself what Joyce had already done in this regard, and she proudly noted how she dug out "beautiful caves" behind her characters, giving them "humour, humanity, depth," the idea being "that the caves shall connect and each comes to daylight at the present moment"—as with Joyce's day-and-night connections in *Ulysses* (*WD*, pp. 60–61). Still, however derivative, the tunneling brought her closer to internal truths, to upwelling memories as they impinge on present life; it made her writing "more analytical and human" than lyrical, and herself more open to the world around her (*WD*, p. 62). Some of the best sequences in the book—the long passage, for instance, in which Clarissa's youthful memories of Peter Walsh and Sally Seton come flooding back when Walsh returns from India—are enriched by the tunneling process with all the depth, humanity, and humor she had groped for. Thanks to Joyce's massive example, she was beginning to join internal with external life in her own authentic way.

It seems evident, however, that the new method had its drawbacks. On the one hand, for all its accessibility, it drew her farther away from common readers than she realized; on the other, it brought her closer to her own "innermost" concerns, or to that "damned egotistical self" which she was not yet willing to confront. Indeed, in this first full-scale application, she came so close to personal problems that she deliberately took a "sidelong approach" to avoid them. She had wanted to write a story about an older family friend, Kitty Maxse, who had died from a fall downstairs at the end of a party, and the story had branched out into a novel. As she disclosed in her Modern Library introduction, she had originally intended that Mrs. Dalloway should die as Kitty Maxse had died, at the end of a party, either by suicide or heart failure. She was inclined toward suicide, in reflection perhaps of her belief that Kitty had thrown herself downstairs rather than fallen to her death (QB 2:87). But after some nine months of labored writing she had abandoned this plan and had devised a double, Septimus Warren Smith, to do the dying for Mrs. Dalloway. Given her own early attempts at suicide (she had thrown herself from a window about four months after her father's death in 1904—this would be Smith's method in the novel; and she had taken an overdose of veronal a year after her marriage to Leonard Woolf), and given too her eventual fate, there is something touching about this confessed evasion: we are asked to accept the author's humble announcement of her choice as "useful" but unimportant information, an indication perhaps of her preference of life over death for her heroine—but at the expense of somebody else's fictive life! Apparently this was how Kitty Maxse's death had affected her—as a propitiation of her own suicidal fears; and from her own reaction, and from Dostoevsky's influence,[7] she had devised her sacrificial double. As many critics note, she had even given him her maiden name, calling him Stephen Smith at one stage of her writing, then naming him anew with nearly sufficient lettering to match her full present name—Septimus Warren

Smith, Virginia Stephen Woolf—and to disperse the name Stephen into a hidden anagram.

We pardon such evasions when they result in fictive gains, and there is much to be said for the gains in *Mrs. Dalloway*. The depiction of Smith's madness is one of the best things of its kind in modern fiction. Painfully recreated out of her own bouts with madness, it conveys with great fidelity the manic and depressive swings she knew firsthand. By juxtaposing this "insane truth" with Mrs. Dalloway's saner vision, she could present aspects of her own mental history with dramatic objectivity, and with admirable artistic honesty. The hazards and consequences of modern alienation come through with compelling force; the dialectic of sanity and insanity is nicely caught. Mrs. Dalloway shares with her double her fear of the sun's heat and the winter's rages, her love of beauty and her sexual coldness, her need for others and her need for privacy, her dreams of grandeur and her dejections, her outward soarings and her inward panics, her homosexual hates and crushes. The alternation between her precarious leanings and his insane extremes, and the implied continuum between them, gives pace and substance to the novel's psychic progress and supports the humanity of both characters. Clarissa's rejected suitor, Peter Walsh, another late addition to the novel's composition, is used with similar effectiveness to establish her nature and to demonstrate her impact upon others. Altogether she becomes one of the most memorable portraits Virginia Woolf would achieve in her new experimental vein; and yet there is a missing dimension in her portrait which may explain why so many readers find her unsatisfactory, and why Virginia Woolf herself found her "tinselly," before inventing her memories, and even then acknowledged her own lingering "distaste" (*WD*, pp. 61, 79).

The usual explanation is her snobbery, her coldness. Virginia Woolf disliked the first quality in Kitty Maxse and the second in herself; but she was too honest in portraying them as aspects of a total person to be faulted here. The explanation runs deeper, I think, and involves her personal avoidances in creating Septimus Smith as Mrs. Dalloway's double. For it is not only suicide she evades thereby, but its basis in Mrs. Dalloway's fictive life, in her unworked grief, guilt, and anger over the death of some beloved person. Septimus Smith is given this burden in the novel, but Mrs. Dalloway is not. Her double is doing something for her she ought to be doing (however sanely) for herself—something she had been intended to do, moreover, in the first version of the novel, but which only exists in the final version in token form.

In "Mrs. Dalloway in Bond Street," the original opening chapter and the story from which the novel began, Clarissa is decidedly more "tinselly," more an object of the author's satiric distaste; but she is also more obsessed with death and mourning and more likely to commit suicide because of it. The story develops, in fact, by counterpoint between her tinselly surface feelings and her growing concern with death, and ends with a flip moment of obtuse bravado: the upright Mrs. Dalloway, in a glove shop on Bond Street, renews a social connection in the face of a violent explosion—a peacetime reminder of the recent war—in the street outside. Nevertheless, the buildup of deathly premonitions and memories of the dead is so strong as to indicate her ultimate confrontation with some past disaster. She is not merely afraid of her own death, as in *Mrs. Dalloway*: she is troubled by her survival of other people's deaths, by the need to go on living without reassuring religious beliefs, and, interestingly, by the wish to escape from mourning others which her own death might afford. Thus it is not Shakespeare's "fear no more the heat o' the sun" which she at first recalls, as in *Mrs. Dalloway*, but Shelley's *Adonais*, as she reflects on a dead friend's reactions to aging, dying, and more frilly matters:

> Middle age is the devil. People like Jack'll never know that, she thought; for he never once thought of death, never, they said, knew he was dying. And now can never mourn—how did it go?—a head grown grey. . . . From the contagion of the world's slow stain. . . . Have drunk their cup a round or two before. . . . From the contagion of the world's slow stain! She held herself upright.
>
> But how Jack would have shouted! Quoting Shelley, in Piccadilly! 'You want a pin,' he would have said. He hated frumps. 'My God Clarissa! My God Clarissa!'—she could hear him now at

the Devonshire House party, about poor Sylvia Hunt in her amber necklace and that dowdy old silk. Clarissa held herself upright for she had spoken aloud. [*MDP*, p. 22]

In chapter 4 of *The Voyage Out* (1915) Clarissa had rapturously quoted the first four lines of the Shelley stanza to another person destined to die young, Rachel Vinrace, and had identified them as lines which at Rachel's age had left her sobbing in the garden. But then, embarrassed by her emotion, she had dismissed the lines by finding "some snuffy old stockbroker" living a mundane life "*really* nobler than poets whom everyone worships just because they're geniuses and die young" (*VO*, p. 55). In this story, then, as in that early novel, her deepest thoughts give way to mundane sentiments and embarrassments. And yet Sylvia Hunt will turn up again as someone who died in Clarissa's youth, "hundreds of years ago," when that prewar garden still seemed simple and lovely and Shelley's poem left her sobbing. Meanwhile there are the fragments of Shelley's poem, which lead ostensibly away from Sylvia's death into narcissistic worries: the dead person escapes mourning his or her lost youth ("a head grown grey"), escapes too the whole process of growing old and ill ("the contagion of the world's slow stain"), and (in a stray line from another poem!) misses only a few rounds of life's comradely satisfactions. Actually the crucial stanza (XI) of Shelley's poem about the death of Keats leads back to the mourning poet's loss of that beloved person:

> He has outsoared the shadow of our night;
> Envy and calumny and hate and pain,
> And that unrest which men miscall delight,
> Can touch him not and torture not again;
> From the contagion of the world's slow stain
> He is secure, and now can never mourn
> A heart grown cold, a head grown grey in vain;
> Nor, when the spirit's self has ceased to burn,
> With sparkless ashes load an unlamented urn.

As the sense of the stanza indicates, the dead Keats has escaped not only the unpleasantnesses of this world, including lost

loves and the spectacle of misspent lives—he has also escaped
having to mourn his unmourned death, escaped then the poet's
lot, the poet's loss, the poet's need to mourn his "unlamented"
and no doubt Grecian "urn." The rest of the poem accordingly
urges that we "mourn not Adonais" but follow where he has fled,
join him in his escape ("Die/If thou wouldst be with that which
thou dost seek"); and there is even the Wordsworthian comfort of
apprehending his spread-out presence in Nature since his death,
which is the only verbal trace of the Shelley poem to recur in *Mrs.
Dalloway*.

Clarissa never consciously develops these implications in
"Mrs. Dalloway in Bond Street." But she unthinkingly keeps re-
peating the key refrains in ways which reinforce them. Thus a
moment later, thinking of a gift she might buy for Hugh Whit-
bread's ailing wife, a woman of her own age, she hits nostalgically
upon Mrs. Gaskell's *Cranford*, with its enchanting humor, its
place for self-respect, its characters who seemed "as if they were
real"—all missing in modern life and art:

> For all the great things one must go to the past, she thought. From
> the contagion of the world's slow stain. . . . Fear no more the heat o'
> the sun. . . . And now can never mourn, can never mourn, she
> repeated, her eyes straying over the [bookstore] window; for it ran
> in her head; the test of great poetry; the moderns had never written
> anything one wanted to read about death, she thought. [*MDP*, p.
> 23]

In *Mrs. Dalloway* the line from Shakespeare's *Cymbeline*,
"Fear no more the heat o' the sun," becomes the heroine's sole
refrain. Its appearance here, within the frame of the discarded
lines from *Adonais*, is accordingly instructive. Clarissa's fears of
death and aging seem to begin with an inability to mourn, or a
desire to escape from mourning, and the removal of this desire will
make a crucial difference in *Mrs. Dalloway*. Meanwhile, in the
"Bond Street" tale, the problem of mourning takes a comic turn as
Clarissa fuses her deeper memories of dowdy Sylvia Hunt with her
surface reaction to a frumpy fellow customer, and with Shelley's
elegy: "It would be intolerable if dowdy women came to her

party! Would one have liked Keats if he had worn red socks?" (*MDP*, p. 26). The question itself makes Clarissa seem frivolous enough; but the implied answer—"not if he were dead"—is anything but frivolous: for she is imagining the dead at her party now, and—if mourning Sylvia as Shelley had mourned Keats means seeking after her—then she is also warding off her own impending suicide with a silly joke. In *Mrs. Dalloway*, as we shall see, the dead Keats will appear at Clarissa's party in two forms: as a radical young poet wearing red socks whose quarrel with a conservative professor she will smooth over, and as a mystic message from the suicidal poet, Septimus Warren Smith; and she will exult in the latter's death, and take courage from his defiance, rather than follow after him.

The next Shelley repetitions in the "Bond Street" tale build somewhat more sympathetically on Clarissa's latent fears. As she thinks now of helping the tired and aging shopgirl in the glove store, then recalls her husband's advice on "the folly of giving impulsively," she compares her plight as an unbeliever with the shopgirl's simple faith:

> And she could feel the girl wouldn't like to be given things. There she was in her place. So with Dick. Selling gloves was her job. She had her own sorrows quite separate, 'and now can never mourn, can never mourn', the words ran in her head, 'From the contagion of the world's slow stain,' thought Clarissa holding her arm stiff, for there are moments when it seems utterly futile (the glove was drawn off leaving her arm flecked with powder)—simply one doesn't believe, thought Clarissa, any more in God. . . .
>
> It used, thought Clarissa, to be so simple. Down, down through the air came the caw of the rooks [as in her childhood at Bourton]. When Sylvia died, hundreds of years ago, the yew hedges looked so lovely with the diamond webs in the mist before early church. But if Dick were to die to-morrow? As for believing in God—no, she would let the children choose, but for herself, like Lady Bexborough, who opened the bazaar, they say, with the telegram in her hand—Roden, her favorite, killed—she would go on. But why, if one doesn't believe? For the sake of others, she thought taking the glove in her hand. The girl would be much more unhappy if she didn't believe. [*MDP*, p. 27]

The shopgirl's imagined separate sorrows remind us of Julia Duckworth Stephen's melancholy grandeur ("She had her own sorrow waiting behind her to dip into privately" [MB, p. 82]) in her children's eyes. Apparently the shopgirl too mourns some beloved person, as Clarissa by implication mourns the lost Sylvia, and from that loss develops an atheist's philosophy of stoic consolation in serving others, as Julia did after her first husband's death, when the utter futility of life gave such service its intense importance. Virginia Woolf, is, quite obviously, half-mocking Clarissa in her adoption of that philosophy: the image of Lady Bexborough opening the bazaar, carrying on with that social triviality upon hearing of her son's death in the war, continues the tale's satiric stress; and Clarissa's impatience with the shopgirl at the end, and her upright posture at the explosion, assuredly completes it. But by then enough weight has been given to the suppressed pain of Sylvia's loss to make us wonder who she is and why she can't be mourned more openly. An early version perhaps of another "untidy" (if not dowdy) person, Sally Seton—that is to say, another adolescent crush—she will appear in a different role in *Mrs. Dalloway*, as Clarissa's gifted sister, Sylvia Parry, whose early death is recounted in fifty-odd words and its impact confined to a long surrounding paragraph. There is no recurrent problem of how to mourn her, how to take her death, what to make of her own failure to grieve so great a loss: that problem is left rather to Mrs. Dalloway's double, who has failed to grieve the death of his wartime friend and superior officer Evans, who thinks continually of his dead friend, talks to him, sees him behind trees and railings or approaching on park paths, and wants to join him in that imperishable world where there is no death—even as Virginia Woolf "saw" and talked with her dead mother for more than thirty years after her death when Virginia was thirteen, when she too failed to grieve at her mother's deathbed. But consider first Clarissa's deathly heritage in the light of the novel's radical revisions.

The opening sentence of "Mrs. Dalloway in Bond Street" is: "Mrs. Dalloway said she would buy the gloves herself." The

opening sentence of *Mrs. Dalloway* is: "Mrs. Dalloway said she
would buy the flowers herself." The slight shift from gloves to
flowers suggests a much more crucial shift in Virginia Woolf's
sympathies for this character, whatever her lingering distaste.
Mrs. Dalloway's love of "life itself" has replaced her social vanity
as the key to her nature; her own outward embraces, of flowers,
gardens, urban flux and bustle, her apprehension of and respect
for the life in other people, have become her salient features. Even
Lady Bexborough's absurd heroic posturing is wrapped now "in
the soft mesh of the grey-blue morning air" (*MD*, pp. 5–6), and the
satiric note itself is by such means muted, subsumed by the life
note. Indeed, Clarissa merely glances in the glove shop window
now, as if to indicate its subordinate position, and passes on to the
flower shop, where her floral raptures overcome the "monster" of
hatred and self-love grubbing at the roots of her soul, and where
she is even allowed to jump at the street explosion outside—that
peacetime reminder of the war's senseless violence.

She is also self-critical now, aware of other people's criti-
cisms of her snobbery and coldness, able to take them into account in her own self-assessment. Her consciousness has been
considerably expanded, then, to allow for an exploration of values Virginia Woolf wants to affirm, prominent among which is
Julia Duckworth Stephen's stoic atheism. Thus, as Peter Walsh
muses over Clarissa's kindnesses to others (seen now as natural
and genuine!), we are given a more affirmative version of her stoic
views and of their source in the senseless death of a beloved person:

> Oddly enough, she was one of the most thoroughgoing
> skeptics he had ever met, and possibly (this was a theory he used to
> make up to account for her, so transparent in some ways, so
> inscrutable in others), possibly she said to herself, As we are a
> doomed race, chained to a sinking ship (her favourite reading as a
> girl was Huxley and Tyndall, and they were fond of these nautical
> metaphors), as the whole thing is a bad joke, let us, at any rate, do
> our part; mitigate the sufferings of our fellow-prisoners (Huxley
> again); decorate the dungeon with flowers and air-cushions; be as
> decent as we possibly can. Those ruffians, the Gods, shan't have it

all their own way,—her notion being that the Gods, who never lost
a chance of hurting, thwarting and spoiling human lives were
seriously put out if, all the same, you behaved like a lady. *That
phase came directly after Sylvia's death—that horrible affair. To
see your own sister killed by a falling tree (all Justin Parry's
fault—all his carelessness) before your very eyes, a girl too on the
verge of life, the most gifted of them, Clarissa always said, was
enough to turn one bitter.* Later she wasn't so positive perhaps; she
thought there were no Gods; no one was to blame; and so she
evolved this atheist's religion of doing good for the sake of goodness. [*MD*, pp. 117–18; italics mine]

   This is all that remains of Virginia Woolf's original impulse
to burden Clarissa with the problem of mourning. She has in fact
given her her mother's early bitterness rather than her own
blocked grief. Through Peter Walsh's increasingly sympathetic
thoughts, moreover, she has endowed her with her mother's
evolving atheistic views (and their likely sources in Huxley and
Tyndall) after her first husband's senseless death; has endowed
her with a father, Judge Justin Parry, modeled upon that fine,
weak, careless barrister, Herbert Duckworth; and, by the same
means in the next paragraph, has endowed her too with her
mother's vitality and good sense during her long second marriage:

   And of course she enjoyed life immensely. It was her nature
   to enjoy. . . . Anyhow there was no bitterness in her [now]; none of
   that moral virtue which is so repulsive in good women. She enjoyed
   practically everything. If you walked with her in Hyde Park now it
   was a bed of tulips, now a child in a perambulator, now some
   absurd little drama she made up on the spur of the moment. (Very
   likely, she would have talked to those lovers, if she had thought
   them unhappy.) She had a sense of comedy that was really exquisite, but she needed people, always people, to bring it out. [*MD*, p.
   118]

   Plainly there is a great deal of Julia Stephen in Clarissa. The
trouble is, the endowment (however briefly indicated) is too
generous; it makes her inconsistent, it contradicts her fears of
approaching death. She ought to be able to accept its approach

calmly, stoically, with a touch of saving humor, as Julia Stephen did; instead she is horrified, jumpy, in constant need of reassurance. Granted, she is fifty-two and has just recovered from a bout with influenza which has whitened her hair and weakened her heart; but Julia Stephen was forty-nine when she died with stoic grace from the same disease. Clarissa's severe anxieties about death would require, I think, a more traumatic source than her sister's early passing, where even the blame is shifted elsewhere, and from which she derives such consoling views: but Virginia Woolf has deprived her of that harsher legacy of unworked grief and incipient insanity which she had herself received from her mother's death, and from her own failure to grieve that death, and which might have explained her heroine's fictive state, and has passed that legacy off instead upon her hapless double. "It's life that matters," she had written in 1924 while turning away from upsurging memories of her mother's death (*DVW* 2:301). For better and for worse, she now turns Clarissa away from similarly disturbing memories and—perhaps for safety's sake—places them at two fictive removes.

Nominally the war is given as the cause of Septimus's madness. A frail, self-educated young man from a poor family, he has come to London to become a poet and clerks there for estate agents. He attends lectures on Shakespeare by Miss Isabel Pole, a lady who likens him to Keats when he writes poems inspired by her, and is "one of the first to volunteer" when the war begins. He develops "manliness" in the war, is promoted, and draws the attention and affection of his superior officer, a man named Evans who is "undemonstrative in the company of women" and with whom he enjoys a kind of rough and tumble puppy love ("They had to be together, share with each other, fight with each other, quarrel with each other"). But when Evans is killed just before the Armistice (he dies like Keats in Italy), "Septimus, far from showing any emotion or recognising that here was the end of a friendship, congratulated himself upon feeling very little and very reasonably." He has been taught by the war, by the code of manliness, to take such tragedies in stride. Then "one evening when

the panic was on him—that he could not feel," he becomes engaged to a young Italian girl, Lucrezia, and begins his descent into
madness (*MD*, pp. 130–31).

Wisely Virginia Woolf does not describe any actual war
experience; she prepares for it instead by something she knows
well enough, the concerned head manager, Mr. Brewer, who in
prewar days advises Smith to take up football for his health. Thus
when war comes, the trenches instantly provide "the change
which Mr. Brewer desired when he advised football" (*MD*, pp.
129–30). She is on the right track, certainly; but as we know from
writers who experienced it firsthand, the war created ironic bitterness and defensive toughness in men which went beyond athle-
tic or military *machismo*, which became in fact a whole new
outlook (witness Hemingway) on the futilities of wasteland life.[8]
Here the component is left to stand (however wisely) for the whole
experience, and we must take it, I think, as a further sign of the
novel's evasion of its own secret causes and of its reliance on
certain stopgap effects for which it fails to provide sufficient
grounds.

Like Nancy Topping Bazin in the quote below, I was once
persuaded that homosexuality was the secret cause of Smith's
absent grief:

> According to Deutsch and Freud, absence of grief may be caused by
> a previously existing conflict with the person who has died. The
> initial failure to experience grief may be due to an unconscious
> wish for that person's death. Septimus' relationship with Evans has
> been that of "two dogs playing on a hearth-rug." His probable
> guilt feelings concerning his sexual attraction to Evans may well
> have made him glad to have death end the relationship. His sub-
> sequent failure to experience grief may have made him feel
> semiresponsible for Evans' death. This seems to explain why, when
> depressed, Septimus is haunted by a sense of guilt.[9]

A plausible hypothesis, certainly, but as I would now like to
contend, without much support from the text. There is no evidence, for example, that Septimus feels guilt about his attraction
to Evans. In fact, the text presents such affections as deeper, truer,
and more purely passionate than heterosexual love, perhaps be-

cause the passions are never consummated. This is the case with Clarissa and Sally Seton, whose sweet garden embrace in youth is set against the predatory passions of Peter Walsh; and it seems to be the case with Smith and Evans, whose innocent rough and tumble is set against the repulsiveness, for Smith as for Shakespeare, of "love between man and woman," the "filth" of copulation and childbirth, the "sordidity" of the human body (*MD*, p. 134). Neither Clarissa nor Smith associates homosexual affections with such "filth." Nor apparently did Virginia Woolf, if we take her diaries and letters and memoirs as evidence: it was heterosexual love which made her feel guilty and unworthy, perhaps because it was *always* intimately carnal.

Septimus starts back in horror, true enough, when he believes Evans is approaching him in Regent's Park: " 'For God's sake don't come!' Septimus cried out. For he could not look upon the dead" (*MD*, p. 105). But when he sees that the approaching man (Peter Walsh!) has no mud on him, no wounds—no signs, perhaps of carnal filth—he rises up with hand raised "like some colossal figure who has lamented the fate of man for ages in the desert alone," and becomes "the giant mourner" who receives with joyous relief an "astonishing revelation" he must announce to the world. As his brief moment of mourning suggests, his quarrel is with the fate of man, with death itself, which—like some devouring carnal rival—has taken away his beloved Evans, but which has now miraculously restored him whole and clean; and in the same vein, his guilt lies not in having wanted Evans to die, but in betraying the pure love between them by failing to mourn his defiling loss. It is for this "crime" and others like it, including his *heterosexual* vices, that he has been condemned to death by "human nature":

> So there was no excuse; nothing whatever the matter, except the sin for which human nature had condemned him to death; that he did not feel. He had not cared when Evans was killed; that was worst; but all the other crimes raised their heads and shook their fingers and jeered and sneered over the rail of the bed in the early hours of the morning at the prostrate body which lay realising its degradation; how he had married his wife without loving her; had

lied to her; seduced her; outraged Miss Isabel Pole, and was so pocked and marked with vice that women shuddered when they saw him in the street. The verdict of human nature on such a wretch was death. [*MD*, pp. 137–38]

Human nature—"the repulsive brute, with the blood-red nostrils" (*MD*, p. 139)— is personified for him by Drs. Holmes and Bradshaw, who treat his malady in terms of physical symptoms and who prescribe physical activities, hobbies, outside interests, for its cure, or when those fail, physical rest. His body, then, is the culprit, and his sense of bodily degradation reminds us of Virginia Woolf's sense of defilement after her half brother Gerald Duckworth's exploration of her "private parts" when she was six. Her lifelong sense of physical shame which began with this incident (and which was later reinforced by the erotic affections of Gerald's older brother George), her inability to mourn at her mother's deathbed at thirteen, and her vision then of death as a carnal (or at the least, incarnate) rival, are transferred now to Mrs. Dalloway's double, whose madness like her own seems to begin with such associated causes. Thus the unworthy Septimus, defiled by previous heterosexual vices, angry with defiling death for depriving him of love, disturbed by the lies and wickedness of "life itself," begins in his madness to reverse these conditions—to exalt himself and to embrace the world and to preach assorted utopian messages, the most important of which are that "there is no crime" and "there is no death" (*MD*, p. 36). It is the loss of love, then, and not the desire to lose it, which has made him angry and unable to mourn, like Virginia Woolf before him.

Part of her problem in composing this novel was her substitution of peers for parents as the loves lost through death. Her first and second breakdowns had occurred, respectively, after her mother's death in 1895 and her father's in 1904; but she had not gone mad when her half sister Stella died in 1897, nor when her brother Thoby died in 1906, nor had she then experienced the same troubles with grieving. Her choice of the sane Clarissa's sister as the lost love may have been appropriate to her sibling experience, if not to Clarissa's later horror of death; but her choice of Evans was not so appropriate, though she does make him the older dog of the playful pair: "one worrying a paper screw, snarling, snapping, giving a pinch, now and then, at the old dog's ear; the other lying somnolent, blinking at the fire, raising a paw, turning and growling good-temperedly" (*MD*, p. 130). Plainly she was moving toward the problem of parental relations she would explore in her next novel, *To the Lighthouse* (1927), where she would finally begin the real work of grieving and so dispel for a time her parental ghosts. But in *Mrs. Dalloway* she was more concerned with the failure of adult loves than with the childhood origins of such failure. And in this sense it is Peter Walsh, and not Sylvia Parry—nor even Sally Seton—whom Clarissa mourns.

Thus, as the novel opens, she is angry with Peter for marrying another woman, for calling Clarissa herself "cold, heartless, a prude," for pursuing "silly, pretty, flimsy nincompoops" who were not so cold, and for wasting his talents in such pursuits (*MD*, pp. 10–11). "Never could she understand how he cared," she says in this context, and so sets the problem before us of the lost possibility of passionate heterosexual love. She has failed her husband, Richard Dalloway, in this regard, and now in her illness sleeps alone on a narrow bed in her own attic room, where she cannot "dispel a virginity preserved through childbirth which clung to her like a sheet" (*MD*, p. 46). Only at times with other women could she feel for a moment what men feel:

(handwritten margin note) 1) Difficulty to display heterosexual love

> It was something central which permeated; something warm which broke up surfaces and rippled the cold contact of man and woman, or of women together. . . . It was a sudden revelation, a tinge like a blush which one tried to check and then, as it spread, one yielded to its expansion, and rushed to the farthest verge and there quivered and felt the world come closer, swollen with some astonishing significance, some pressure of rapture, which split its thin skin and gushed and poured with an extraordinary alleviation over the cracks and sores! [*MD*, pp. 46–47]

But such poetic intimations of sexual rapture are soon over: "the close withdrew; the hard softened"; and she retires once more to her narrow bed, to review in her mind her youthful love for Sally Seton and its shocking interruption by jealous, predatory, hostile Peter Walsh (*MD*, pp. 48–53). Yet it is Walsh, and not Sally, who possesses her imagination like a lost chance. She owes him touchstone words like "sentimental" and "civilised," which "started up every day of her life as if he guarded her" (*MD*, p. 54). She also argues often with him in her mind, perhaps because she wants "his good opinion" of her, but chiefly, it seems, to prove "that she had been right . . . not to marry him" (*MD*, p. 10). For in marriage, she believes, some independence must obtain between people living closely together—this "Richard gave her, and she him": "But with Peter everything had to be shared; everything gone into. And it was intolerable, and when it came to that scene in the little garden by the fountain, she had to break with him or they would have been destroyed, both of them ruined, she was convinced; though she had borne about with her for years like an arrow sticking in her heart the grief, the anguish" (*MD*, p. 10).

It is Peter Walsh, then, whom she has lost to women who better understand male passion, whom she mourns. It is Peter Walsh whom she has given up, because—like those soul-forcers Drs. Holmes and Bradshaw who violate the privacy of the self in the hapless Smith—he would have violated her integrity of being, her intact virginity.[10] Peter is her version of that repulsive brute with blood-red nostrils, human nature, and of that sexual and spiritual defilement it demands—that passionate and penetrating and soul-destroying love. And yet she opens up his deepest feelings, understands him as no one else does, communicates with him without words; and—when he returns sooner than expected from India and weeps before her unashamedly—she feels a tropic gale of silver plumes flashing and brandishing in her breast, glimpses in one moment the gaiety of their potential married life together, wants impulsively to be taken away by him, then imagines she has already lived that lifetime, has run off and lived with him, and that it is now all over like an exciting five-act play (*MD*, pp. 69–70). "The death of the soul"—Peter had ticketed her prudishness in the old days (*MD*, pp. 88–89). But it is his soul, not hers, which has run to seed in running after silly nincompoops.

Meanwhile she has kept herself worthy and intact, first by refusing his violating love, now, by dismissing its passionate closeness as a moving piece of theatre—exciting but unreal. In any case, she is now too old for it: "It was all over for her. The sheet was stretched and the bed narrow. She had gone up to the tower alone and left them blackberrying in the sun" (*MD*, p. 70).

It is characteristic of this novel, and of Virginia Woolf's art, that we are given three alternatives and not allowed to choose between them: passionate love for Clarissa would violate the privacy of the soul; it would also be gaily exciting and liberating, but as an imaginative romp best left untested by reality; and it would have been, quite simply, blackberrying in the sun. All these propositions seem to be equally true, if, like Clarissa, we cannot "say of any one in the world now that they were this or were that" (*MD*, p. 11). But we can say something, nonetheless, about the displacement of romantic love in her creator's fiction. One way or another, after *Night and Day* (1919), it remains out of reach for all her questing characters; and in *Mrs. Dalloway* we begin to see why this is so.

It is the death of romantic love which Clarissa mourns in mourning Peter Walsh, and she is quite relieved to be rid of it. She has settled this problem for herself by 11:30 a.m. on the day of her party, one quarter of the way through the novel; and she will not take it up again until 3:30 p.m., when we see her confirmed in her old position, that love, like religion, is a horrible and degrading passion which destroys everything that is fine and true (*MD*, p. 192). By this point she is fairly certain, as she watches the old woman in the opposite house climbing upstairs, that sexual passion is a form of the sun's heat she need not fear, that there are other ways of surviving, that the "privacy of the soul" is the supreme miracle and mystery which she must preserve at all costs (*MD*, pp. 192–93).

Romantic love seems to be one of those costs. It had died for her creator, I think, with the deaths of her mother and her older half sister, Stella Duckworth, whose maternal counsel she sorely longed for in her youth. In *Night and Day*, for instance, Katherine Hilbery can only achieve it through the intercession of her literary mother, vaguely wise and reassuring, calling for faith in her vision of love. Clarissa Dalloway has no such faith, and though old Mrs.

Hilbery appears briefly at her party, it is only to reassure herself "on a point which sometimes bothered her if she woke up early in the morning and did not like to call her maid for a cup of tea; how it is certain we must die" (*MD*, p. 267). Interestingly, she takes this reassurance from a story of the music hall stage ("about the Duke and the Lady") which the venerable Academician Sir Harry has just told to some male cronies and has refused to repeat to Clarissa—a lady so refined he finds it impossible to ask her to sit on his knee, though plainly he would like to. But "that wandering will-o'-the-wisp, that vagulous phosphorescence, old Mrs. Hilbery," as Sir Harry sees her, has heard this exclusive bit of male bawdy from across the room, and the inference she draws from it ("stretching her hands to the blaze of his laughter") seems to be that, given this male refusal of women's feelings—especially older women's feelings—about the blazing passions, she might as well prepare for death. In her conversation with Clarissa, which directly follows, Mrs. Hilbery may be transferring her odd reassurance on this point in a positive way, for she seems to be saying that at least Clarissa's long-dead mother took the point with old-world grace:

> "They won't tell us their stories," said Clarissa.
> "Dear Clarissa!" exclaimed Mrs. Hilbery. She looked to-night, she said, so like her mother as she first saw her walking in a garden in a grey hat.
> And really Clarissa's eyes filled with tears. Her mother, walking in a garden! But alas, she must go. [*MD*, p. 267]

She goes, as mentioned earlier, to smooth over an impending quarrel between a conservative professor and a bad if radical young poet wearing red socks—the first sign of Keats at her party! (*MD*, p. 268). But whether she goes with any reassurance about facing death is uncertain. She has briefly mourned her dead mother in that telltale Shelleyan garden of the past, and she has done so without those defilements which apparently made Virginia Woolf feel unworthy at the time of her own mother's death; but she has also done so at the cost of lifelong virginity. Thus her own sexual refusal now matches the refusal of the male enclave. She excludes herself from what she is in any case excluded.

So, I think, does Virginia Woolf. In her forties as she wrote this novel, she was as much aware of the blackberrying she had foregone as of the male tyranny as to the proper female age for blackberrying or the proper audience for sexist tales about it. And so she gives us Clarissa, on the one hand, behaving "like a virgin protecting chastity, respecting privacy," and on the other, Peter Walsh pursuing a young woman through the park, a British Leopold Bloom enjoying his bit of male chauvinist fantasy. But as for blackberrying itself, we are given only a few yearnings, a few set pieces—Clarissa "standing in her bedroom at the top of the house holding the hotwater can in her hands and saying aloud [of Sally Seton], 'She is beneath this roof . . . She is beneath this roof!" (*MD*, p. 51), or Clarissa imagining what men feel, the swollen pressure which gushes and pours over cracks and sores (*MD*, p. 47), or feeling her tropic gale of flashing plumes as she comforts the weeping predator, Peter Walsh (*MD*, p. 69). And, opposed to all this, we are given the passionless affection she enjoys with. Richard Dalloway, who brings her flowers, thinks rather than voices his love, and keeps his respectful distance. There is nowhere in this novel, nor anywhere else in her mature fiction, that union of the passions and affections by which adult romantic love usually proceeds; there are only predatory passions on the one hand, and respectful or gallant affections on the other. It is thus a Victorian standoff, a Victorian impasse, for all its modern sexual frankness.

And with Virginia Woolf even that frankness is a curious mixture of masculine toughness, on the one hand, and feminine evasion on the other. Though she was relieved by the frank language of the private Bloomsbury circle, she was shocked by the public presence of sexual thoughts and terms in Joyce's *Ulysses* and made it a point to avoid such "filth" in her own fiction. Thus adultery and infidelity occur offstage, lesbianism and homosexuality appear as puppy love, male masturbation fantasy becomes playing with a pocketknife, and passion itself—always unconsummated—exists only as poetic metaphor. Indeed, in the

Dalloway stories which accompanied and followed the book she uses euphemisms for the mildest sexual references, such as *"that"* for menopause; and in *Mrs. Dalloway* itself, as in later novels, she tends to suppress such allusions or to delete even those she attempts.[11]

Woolf tried courageously, all the same, to deal with sexuality as part of human suffering and human comedy, and of the ongoing struggle, in modern times, for human dignity and fulfillment. She knew abstractly that it had to be taken into account, and further that it ought to reflect the intimacy and fullness of her own bodily experience. But like so many women writers since her time, she had learned only to use it as men tend to use it, that is to say, defensively, as a convenient province from which the feminine affections are excluded—as a masculine cover, then, for her own failure to love, or to get at the sources of that failure in her unworked grief and childhood shame.

Thus, in a late essay, "Professions for Women," she constructs a similar masculine cover for her inability to express her "own experiences as a body" (*CE* 2:288). As a woman writer, she tells us, she was able to slay the Angel in the House, the unselfish, self-sacrificing, and, above all, pure woman of the past who "never had a mind or a wish of her own, but preferred to sympathize always with the minds and wishes of others," and who accordingly urged her when she wrote to flatter, sympathize, deceive, to use all the indirect arts and wiles of her sex, to keep her own mind hidden, and above all to be pure (*CE* 2:285). This woman she killed after a long hard struggle (though as we have seen, her unselfishness, purity, and tea-table indirection in fact persist in the common selfless voice of the mature fiction). But she could not kill the male opponent to sexual frankness in a woman writer—let us call him the Tyrant in the House, though she does not, and make no bones about the abstracted presence here of Leslie as well as Julia Stephen. This Tyrant appears, then, as she posits a young woman writer fishing "the depths of our unconscious being," her imaginative line rushing to "the pools, the depths, the dark places where the largest fish slumber," when suddenly there is a "smash," "an explosion," "foam and confusion":

The imagination had dashed itself against something hard . . . To speak without figure, she had thought of something, something about the body, about the passions which it was unfitting for her as a woman to say. Men, her reason told her, would be shocked. The consciousness of what men will say of a woman who speaks the truth about her passions had roused her from her artist's state of consciousness. She could write no more. . . . This I believe to be a very common experience with women writers—they are impeded by the extreme conventionality of the other sex. For though men sensibly allow themselves great freedom in these respects, I doubt that they realize or can control the extreme severity with which they condemn such freedom in women. [CE 2:287–88]

The point is decidedly well-taken; the fisherwoman (who is called "a fisherman") has snagged her line on some rocklike submersion of the male superego. Still, the personal sources of this metaphor, in that explosive man of reason and extreme conventionality, Sir Leslie Stephen, whose extended life would have stopped Virginia from writing, render it a little suspect. Certainly the men in her Bloomsbury circle would have met sexual frankness of this kind with approval, and in fact some of her memoirs for that private circle are much franker than her public fiction. But they are frank in a hard masculine way, that is to say without much affect, without much feeling, and this is also true of some of her later fiction, her sexual disclosures in *The Years*, for instance, about Colonel Pargiter. Would it be fairer to say, then, that just as Virginia Woolf emulates her father as a critic and reviewer, but with something like her mother's indirection, so in her fiction she combines masculine hardness about sex—always predatory in men—with feminine evasion of its value for women? Her modesty before male conventionality may be part of her feminine inhibition—but even the prudish Clarissa wants to join the male enclave, and there is something masculine, after all, about doing in the Angel in the House so as to speak your own mind—witness, the tyrannical Mr. Ramsay in *To the Lighthouse*.

Recent critics have ignored these signs of parental influence and have traced Woolf's sexual inhibitions to that disastrous first year of marriage when Leonard's complicity in her sexual fears contributed to her third and fourth breakdowns and to her second

attempt at suicide.[12] Though their case for Leonard's complicity is
persuasive, it seems to me a mistake to cast him as the villain who
denied her both sexual fulfillment and the chance to bear children
at this time. Her own complicity in these deprivations was at least
as great as Leonard's and she seems to have considered it far
greater. When she endows Clarissa Dalloway with "a virginity
preserved through childbirth which clung to her like a sheet," she
may well be acknowledging her own cold reaction to the idea of
childbirth. When she tells us further that Clarissa "failed" her
husband, first at Clieveden, then at Constantinople, "and again
and again" thereafter (*MD*, p. 46), she may well be admitting her
own sexual coldness in the early years with Leonard. If those
disastrous years confirmed and sealed her coldness, they yield no
evidence of Leonard's determining role in producing it. He did put
her into the hands of obtuse neurologists whose extreme physical
regimen she violently resisted; but between 1916 and 1941—the
most productive years of her career—his milder ministrations of
that regimen seem to have kept her going. As their mutual accommodation in these years attests, she bore him no grudges as
either the producer or sealer of her coldness. If her portrait of
Richard Dalloway offers valid testimony, she even ranked
Leonard among those who respect the soul's privacy, cheerfully
settle for companionate love, and do not include themselves
among the reproving male enclave.

I would trace her inhibitions, rather, to the double messages
she received in childhood and adolescence about men, and to her
inability to find *women* who would share her feelings and
help her to sort them out. The legends she grew up with of her
mother's first romantic marriage to Herbert Duckworth, and her
apparent hallucination of a ghostly reunion with that first and
rightful lover—the man at the edge of her mother's deathbed—as
placed against her several violations by his sons, the brothers
Duckworth, is one such double message; and her romantic view of
the marriage of Stella Duckworth and Jack Hills, as placed against
his supposedly wholesome attempt to inform her that most men
trifle with women, is another—no doubt compounded by the
family scandal, after Stella's death, over Jack's attachment to her
consoling sister Vanessa. With no help possible from those dead

Angels in the House, Julia and Stella, Virginia Woolf's faith in romantic love was inevitably shortlived, and with it went that union of the passions and affections she veritably *longed* to uphold. What remained was the hard case against predatory male passion and her lifelong sense of bodily defilement—male-inflicted, of course, but a more likely snag for unconscious depths than her father's social disapproval (his masculine *hardness* is another matter) or her husband's complicity in sexual failure. In any case, she could not express her sexual feelings, nor connect them with her affections, because a series of family disasters had reinforced her early physical shame and bottled up her love for her ungrieved mother—and with it her abiding confidence in herself as a lovable and attractive woman, a sexual self worth loving.

In her next novel, *To the Lighthouse*, she would at least release that love and make some progress in the real work of grieving. Meanwhile, in *Mrs. Dalloway*, that work is temporarily evaded or, at best, displaced. Clarissa lives through her double's suicide as vicariously as she had lived through her potential marriage to Peter Walsh; she understands at once, when she receives the Keatsian news at her party, that he has done it to escape violation of the soul's privacy, and she draws from it the mystic message of defiance, the embrace of preserved integrity of being—without any confrontation at all of that unworked burden of grieving, loss, defilement, guilt, and anger which her hapless double has had to bear for her, and of that telltale inability to feel which makes her own defense of the soul's privacy so suspect and her vision of an old woman going quietly to bed so falsely reassuring (*MD*, p. 283). This burden makes more sense, incidentally, as a cause for suicide than defiance of two cardboard doctors—the only major characters in the novel without real interiority—against whose practice of Conversion, or Soul-Forcing, the author sermonizes for five indignant pages in her common selfless tea-table voice! (*MD*, pp. 149–54).[13] It is—to put it bluntly—a psycho-literary copout, this vicarious refusal to mourn, and though readers common and uncommon may not mind it, for me at least it spoils the intended shared excitement of the novel's ending, as Peter Walsh for the third time reacts to the mystery of Clarissa's presence as an intact, inviolable, selfless being with the magic formula: "It is Clarissa.... For there she was" (MD, pp. 74, 115, 296). She was not there, certainly, when the real grieving was blocked and the real dying and/or defying done, and so we may legitimately ask, at least of the closing lines—Where? Where? Where?

One answer, of course, is a crucial step closer to her spinsterly successor, Lily Briscoe, in To the Lighthouse. If we take these successive novels as stages in Woolf's ongoing struggle with her own internal problems, then Clarissa's spinsterly intactness—however shaky, however dubiously achieved—was a hard-won triumph. From it Woolf received the reassurance she needed to confront impacted grief more directly in the novel ahead, through a character who needs no double to do her grieving. To exist on a continuum with that more credibly engaged survivor is a not unworthy literary fate, though as we shall see there are questions about Lily's motives for mourning, and about the curiously unmotivated sadness of the woman whose death she mourns, which give even sharper focus to those I have raised about Clarissa and her double.

5 Lily Briscoe's Borrowed Grief

With mother's death the merry, various family life which she had held in being shut for ever. In its place a dark cloud settled over us; we seemed to sit all together cooped up, sad, solemn, unreal, under a haze of heavy emotion. It seemed impossible to break through. It was not merely dull; it was unreal. A finger seemed laid on one's lips.

I see us now, all dressed in unbroken black, George and Gerald in black trousers, Stella with real crape deep on her dress, Nessa and myself with slightly modified crape, my father black from head to foot—even the notepaper was so black bordered that only a little space for writing remained—I see us emerging from Hyde Park Gate on a fine summer afternoon and walking in procession hand in hand, for we were always taking hands—I see us walking—I rather proud of the solemn blackness and the impression it must make—into Kensington Gardens; and how golden the laburnum shone. And then we sat silent under the trees. The silence was stifling. A finger was laid on our lips. One had always to think whether what one was about to say was the right thing to say. It ought to be a help. But how could one help? Father used to sit sunk in gloom. If he could be got to talk—and that was part of our duty—it was about the past. It was about "the old days". And when he talked, he ended with a groan.

Moments of Being (pp. 93–94)

Four times during the conception, writing, and publishing of *To the Lighthouse* Virginia Woolf expressed in her diaries her fear of the book's sentimentality. Thus, on Monday, July 20, 1925, even before the actual writing had begun, she was arming herself against that hazard:

The word "sentimental" sticks in my gizzard (I'll write it out of me in a story—Ann Watkins of New York is coming on Wednesday to enquire about my stories). But this theme may be sentimental; father and mother and child in the garden; the death; the sail to the Lighthouse. I think, though, that when I begin it I shall enrich it in all sorts of ways; thicken it; give it branches—roots which I do not perceive now. It might contain all characters boiled down; and

75

> then this impersonal thing, which I'm dared to do by my friends,
> the flight of time and the consequent break of unity in my design.
> That passage . . . interests me very much. A new problem like that
> breaks fresh ground in one's mind; prevents the regular ruts.
> [*WD*, pp. 80–81]

Diffusely anxious in this entry, she offers three solutions for
sentimentality where one might do: she will expel it from her
gizzard by writing another story, a kind of purging of emotions
which now possess her; she will master it, in the novel itself, by
enrichment, thickening, getting into the essentials of characteri-
zation and of childhood—the method which I. A. Richards pre-
scribes, in *Practical Criticism*, of actualizing and disinfecting
charged material by working it into a rich living context;[1] and,
finally, she will overcome it by technical experiment—an impersonal passage on the flight of time—as if an aesthetic exercise of
this kind might dissolve its potency or release its hold through
distancing and novelty.

The second entry, on Sunday, September 5, 1926, comes
near the end of the writing process:. "The lyric portions of *To the
Lighthouse* are collected in the 10-year lapse and don't interfere
with the text so much as usual. I feel as if it fetched its circle pretty
completely this time; and I don't feel sure what the stock criticism
will be. Sentimental? Victorian?" (*WD*, p. 100).

As the passage indicates, her old lyric manner now seems
suspect; she has tried to confine it to the impersonal "Time Passes"
section, as if by lyric uplift alone she might overshoot the sentimental hazards of the deaths she here bypasses, or at least might
isolate them from the preceding and concluding sections which she
identifies, interestingly, as "the text." By the fourth entry she will
have even more severe doubts about this middle section. Meanwhile she is still diffusely afraid of being charged with Victorianism,
or sentimentality, in dealing at all with the emotions of family life
and childhood. Thus, a week later, on Monday, September 13,
1926, she repeats her dread of the theme itself: "And this last lap, in
the boat, is hard, because the material is not so rich as it was with
Lily on the lawn. I am forced to be more direct and more intense. I
am making more use of symbolism, I observe; and I go in dread of

'sentimentality'. Is the whole theme open to that charge? But I doubt that any theme is in itself good or bad. It gives a chance to one's peculiar qualities—that's all" (*WD*, p. 101).

The confession that she has *not* been so direct and intense with the richer material of Lily's liberating grief on the lawn, which enables her to complete her painting and have her "vision," is matter for *our* theme, if not hers: she has been avoiding the emotional hazards of her material by indirections when it is rich, by symbolism when it thins out and forces more direct confrontations. Her "peculiar qualities"—among them her romantic soarings and polite evasions—continue to be as Victorian as she fears, though passed off here as the personal side of her impersonal artistry.

The fourth entry, on May 5, 1927, moves from the exultation of publication and sales to the old fear of reviewers:

> Book out. We have sold (I think) 1690 before publication—twice *Dalloway*. I write however in the shadow of the damp cloud of *The Times Lit. Sup.* review, which is an exact copy of the *J.'s R.*, *Mrs. Dalloway* review, gentlemanly, kindly, timid, praising beauty, doubting character, and leaving me moderately depressed. I am anxious about "Time Passes." Think the whole thing may be pronounced soft, shallow, insipid, sentimental. Yet, honestly, I don't much care; want to be let alone to ruminate. [*WD*, pp. 106–7]

She has been given the Victorian treatment by the *Times Literary Supplement* and, understandably, it rankles—enough so to move her to confess her fear that the "Time Passes" section, designed to avoid sentimentality through impersonalism, is in fact a soft, insipid, shallow specimen of that dread disease. And yet on Friday, January 14, 1927, on revising the completed manuscript for her husband Leonard to read, she had felt that it was "a hard muscular book"— that it had "not run out and gone flabby"— "which at this age proves that I have something in me" (*WD*, p. 103).

Hard, muscular, unflabby. Was she as tough now as her mountain-climbing father, on whose character the book was originally supposed to center? Or was she as soft, insipid, and shallow as he sometimes saw her mother? One is reminded here of the somewhat different opposition in *Mrs. Dalloway* between "civilised" and "sentimental," those verbal touchstones which Peter Walsh bequeaths to Clarissa as daily guardians in a hostile world. Walsh probably derived those touchstones, along with other qualities (his obtuseness to the feelings of others, his unwarranted rages and emotional outpourings, his analytic probings and impossible demands), from that late-Victorian gentleman, Leslie Stephen, who also (whatever his own brutal rages) believed in civilized conduct in a godless world, and who also (whatever his own outpourings) "had no use for optimism, cant, gush, enthusiasm."[2] But Virginia Woolf had acquired her own "civilised qualities"—restraint, sympathy, unselfishness (*MB*, p. 129)— from her hostessing years for her Victorian father, and plainly she had absorbed his relatively dry brand of skepticism at an early age. Did she come armed, then, with his masculine weapons— hard impersonal muscular analytic artistry—as well as their civilized feminine complement—restraint, sympathy, unselfishness—in facing up to the dread sentimentality, the overwhelming feelings and the shameful things they shielded, of her own childhood attachments to both parents? Certainly the writing of this book would release her for a time, as we know, from her obsessive daily dealings with these watchful specters. But would it wholly free her from things hidden by their sentimental shrouds?

We can see from her own childhood recollections why her release was only partial, if much needed and courageously achieved. Her portraits of her parents in Mr. and Mrs. Ramsay are as significant in their evasions and exclusions as in their confrontations. Indeed, the scene itself is not the Cornwall coastal town of her childhood, St. Ives, but the Isle of Skye in western Scotland, which she would not even visit until the summer of 1938, over ten years after completing the novel. The size of the Ramsay family is the same as her own, two parents and eight children, four boys and four girls: but they are children by the same two parents! The whole Victorian ménage of children from three families—Leslie Stephen's retarded Laura from his first marriage to Minny Thackeray; Julia Stephen's Stella, George, and Gerald from her first marriage to Herbert Duckworth; and Julia and Leslie's Vanessa,

Thoby, Virginia, and Adrian from their own marriage—has been sacrificed for the sake of artistic economy; and by that strategic sacrifice the whole hothouse problem of predatory trifling by the Duckworth boys with their young half sisters, with its lifelong damage to Virginia, has been avoided. So too has the source of Mrs. Ramsay's stoic atheism—her brave searching radiance in the face of suffering, death, the poor, unhappiness, treachery, unreason, disorder, injustice. Unlike Julia Stephen, she has no personal tragedy, no "perfect" first marriage ending in a husband's sudden death, no eight years of widowhood with three young children, to explain "the sternness at the heart of her beauty" which her fictive husband notes, and that saddening "remoteness" from himself and others which makes him feel unable to "protect her" (*TTL*, p. 98). Then too, by leaving out the details of her mother's death, of her own subsequent breakdown, and of Stella Duckworth's death soon after, the funereal gloom and emotional distress which possessed and repossessed the family in "the 10-year lapse" is lost, and with it the substantiality and force of Leslie Stephen's most outlandish rages, his constant demands upon his daughters for attention and sympathy, and their own outraged sufferance of his tyranny.

Would the novel be improved by the inclusion of such family disasters? Or would their empirical densities and progressions produce a different kind of fiction? Certainly when Virginia Woolf turned to them in her most popular novel, *The Years* (1937), she produced a hopeless mélange of family complications, a historical dreamfloat of lyric impressions and "cotton wool" realities, as she would later call them (*MB*, p. 70). Of course, the material itself did not insure artistic success; and in any case she had legitimately chosen, in *To the Lighthouse*, to convey the essence rather than the substance of Victorianism, and did so with moving power. Still, the novel's depth as an elegy, its poignance as a grieving, its cathartic force as a release from childhood suffering, might have been increased by some fictive coping with these terrible events; some of its disguises and effusions might have been avoided; and its more dubious borrowings from the author's life might have been paid for in good fictive coin.

Consider in this light the odd placement of the artist, Lily

Briscoe, whom Woolf modeled nominally upon her sister Vanessa but more substantially upon herself. Lily is thirty-three as the novel opens in mid-September, shortly before the first World War—a year or so older than Virginia in the fall of 1913. She is cast as a friend of the Ramsay family, and is said to love the whole family; but like Virginia, she has lost a mother, and her affections for Mrs. Ramsay—like Virginia's affections for older women after her mother's death—are especially intense. Through Lily, then, Virginia returns to her own family as a motherless woman in her thirties, and her reactions to Mrs. Ramsay are like those of an actual daughter once removed. It is Lily, for instance, who grieves openly for Mrs. Ramsay near the novel's close, some ten years after her death—which would be in 1924, about the time Virginia Woolf conceived this novel. A spinster lady who likes to paint, who seems repelled by the very sexuality which attracts her, and who steadfastly resists Mrs. Ramsay's urgings that she should marry, she is like the other characters "boiled down" to such reactions. There is no attempt to account for them by the kind of sexual trifling the author endured in childhood and again in young adulthood; nor by the double messages about men and marriage which she then received, and which are here reduced to a social issue without much psychological depth. They receive no emotional reinforcement, moreover, from Mrs. Ramsay's death, as they obviously did for Virginia Woolf, for the immediate impact of that death is whisked away by "the flight of time."

The only other appropriate character who might have received that impact is the youngest daughter, Cam, who is seven when the novel begins. Virginia Woolf was about that age when she was molested by her eighteen-year-old half brother, Gerald Duckworth, and so derived her lifelong sense of bodily shame. Cam, more fortunately, is frightened only by a boar's skull at night, an uncle's gift which the children have nailed to the bedroom wall, over which her comforting mother throws a disguising shawl and around which she weaves beautiful images—"it was like a bird's nest; it was like a beautiful mountain . . . with valleys and flowers and bells ringing and birds singing and little goats and antelopes and . . . everything lovely" (*TTL*, p. 172)—until she gradually falls asleep. There is some poignance here in the greater sternness of Julia Stephen's last words to Virginia, which one of these phrases echoes: "Hold yourself straight, my little Goat" (*MB*, p. 84)—as if it were up to her to meet boars bravely, without maternal comfort, in the years to come. Cam is more swathingly protected, then, against the "great horns" of approaching death, and perhaps also of defiling sexuality; she feels no need to grieve, some ten years later, when she takes the trip to the Lighthouse with her father and is preoccupied instead with *his* death-defying ways. But Virginia Woolf did feel the need to grieve, and through Lily Briscoe (to whom she gives no psychic history) she tried to meet it bravely enough for most human purposes, in her own belated way—the way of therapeutic elegy—with all the main chords muted.

Or perhaps all but one. The "centrality" of Mrs. Ramsay, her "general presence" as the center of family life, is very much the novel's subject. As noted, Virginia Woolf's initial impulse had been to center the book on her father's character; but her governing image of him "sitting in a boat, reciting We perished, each alone, while he crushes a dying mackerel" (*WD*, p. 77), threatened to reduce his stoic posing to sentimental viciousness by the novel's end. She would nonetheless "have father's character done complete" in the novel, and almost as an afterthought, "mother's" (*WD*, p. 76). The case for her greater concern with her father is an old one, much abetted by Quentin Bell's recent biography, with its early account of Virginia jumping about naked in the bathroom with her sister Vanessa, asking her which parent she liked best, and, when Vanessa promptly said her mother, deciding "after much delay and deliberation . . . that she preferred her father" (*QB*, 1:26). In *Woman of Letters* (p. 112) Phyllis Rose takes this hesitant decision as an early instance of rebellion; but my own impression is that Vanessa's forthright answer must have stopped Virginia cold. In her self-defeating childhood lottery, her father was the only parent left to prefer; as indeed he was when he outlived her mother and her delayed (and perhaps unwanted) preference was further overlaid by circumstance. She would of course emulate him in her career, especially in her critical writing, and as we have just speculated, in her desire for tough unsentimental muscular effects in her fiction. But the strength to emulate him came, as I hope now to show, from Julia Stephen, and the awareness of his tyrannical nature came from Julia too, as did the ability to love him whenever he showed himself capable of loving anyone else except his mackerel-crushing self.

It was to Julia Stephen, then, whom Virginia turned in the actual writing of the novel, giving her the inner fullness she could not imagine for her father, endowing her character rather than his with mystery, richness, creativity, and making of her empathetic desire to send presents to the Lighthouse the novel's moving impulse. Her prototype, Mrs. Ramsay, has more interiority and more substance than any other character, including the appreciative and critical Miss Briscoe, who must learn to grieve her before she can "want" Mr. Ramsay as the novel ends. It is Mrs. Ramsay, Lily thinks, who holds the secret of life, in whose mind and heart "tablets bearing sacred inscriptions" might be found which "would teach one everything" (*TTL*, pp. 78–79); it is she whom Lily must learn to love if she too is to have her vision of "life itself."

Interestingly, Mrs. Ramsay does not stand in any fundamental opposition to her husband as to the nature of life, as some critics hold, but only in how to respond to it. Both husband and wife are stoic pessimists and stalwart copers with a godless world. If anything, she is more pessimistic than he in wanting to keep the children locked into the happy childhood world she makes for them and so denying the bleak future he cheerfully accepts (*TTL*, p. 91). But where Ramsay sees himself as the failed but heroic leader of brave expeditions, the bold confronter of grim realities about which he is basically optimistic, she sees herself as a fount of supportive sympathy and reassurance, of empathetic appreciation and renewal, in a world of constantly impending tragedy. They need one another, moreover, if they are to fulfill their chosen roles; they depend on one another, in loving if excessive ways, to insure their complementary functions; and their intimacy is so great they sometimes "read" one another by their inverse meanings. Thus, if Ramsay is a draining and demanding egotist, and his wife is vain and self-destructive in her unselfish giving, she nevertheless depends on him as much for his grim reproofs to her pessimism (e.g., *TTL*, p. 184) as he depends on her for sympathy as a fallen hero. The question, however, is not so much how they relate to each other, or even how they fare in their own lives, but what they have to give to their children—the heritage of the past which may be salvaged from their complementary natures as stranded voyagers. And here Mrs. Ramsay—who is emotionally and socially creative where he is merely effective in academic circles, a climber of mental mountains, a master of the philosphic alphabet up to the letter R—plainly has the most to offer.

At that point in the novel where Lily sits with her head in Mrs. Ramsay's lap, her arms around her knees, and wants above all unity, intimacy, oneness with this adored guardian of life's secret wisdom, we see the maternal sources of Mrs. Ramsay's power (*TTL*, pp. 78–79). The selfless oneness she promises is like that maternal sharing of the world's surrounding richness by which every life is or should be launched.[3] It is like that feeling of "lying in a grape and seeing through a film of semi-transparent yellow" (*MB*, p. 65) which Virgina Woolf so cherished in her childhood; a feeling then of womblike security and selfless rapture by which selfhood is initially nourished, and from which it may then develop toward confident independent being. The characters who come to Mrs. Ramsay for this enveloping maternal reassurance range from the eight children who deserve it as their birthright to the full complement of adult admirers who renew their sense of themselves at her maternal fount. Only a few of these adult characters—Augustus Carmichael, William Bankes, and perhaps in retrospect, Lily Briscoe—partake of these healing waters with anything like consistent reciprocity and selfless exchange: for Mrs. Ramsay has few equals. Her children, as indicated, have the right to her renewing reassurances without equal return; but her husband, whose constant demands for sympathy and replenishment epitomize the usual adult tribute to her powers, does not. This is the problem with which the novel opens and which, I think, it never wholly solves.

The youngest child, James, wants to go to the Lighthouse on the following day, a wondrous expedition to which he has looked forward "for years and years, it seemed" (*TTL*, p. 9). His mother says "Yes, of course, if it's fine tomorrow." His father says "it won't be fine." James wants to kill his father with an axe or poker: "Such were the extremes of emotion that Mr. Ramsay excited in his children's breasts by his mere presence; standing, as now lean as a knife, narrow as the blade of one, grinning sarcastically, not only with the pleasure of disillusioning his son and casting ridicule upon his wife, who was ten thousand times better in every way than he was (James thought), but also with some secret conceit at his own accuracy of judgement" (*TTL*, p. 10).

As the passage makes clear, the problem is not what Mr. Ramsay says, but how and why he says it. He is delivering a judgment which redounds to his own credit and which, by his whole manner of delivery, discredits others. He is the academic critic par excellence, and in the nominally digressive action which shortly follows, in which Mrs. Ramsay takes his admiring and parodic disciple, Charles Tansley, on an errand of charity in town, the point is underscored by her memory of the children's complaint, that Tansley turns everything interesting they talk about into something which reflects well upon himself and disparages them (*TTL*, p. 16). The question, then, is not about the weather, or the true nature of things, though Mrs. Ramsay does hold out (at least nominally) for better weather, but about how to take life's grim realities. Still, there is a parental point at stake in Mr. Ramsay's nastiness:

> What he said was true. It was always true. He was incapable of untruth; never tampered with a fact; never altered a disagreeable word to suit the pleasure or convenience of any mortal being, least of all his own children, who, sprung from his loins, should be aware from childhood that life is difficult; facts uncompromising; and the passage to that fabled land where our brightest hopes are extinguished, our frail barks founder in darkness (here Mr. Ramsay would straighten his back and narrow his little blue eyes upon the horizon), one that needs, above all, courage, truth, and the power to endure. [*TTL*, pp. 10–11]

The parental aim is sensible enough, and Mrs. Ramsay even agrees with it, if we may apply to her Julia Stephen's final words to Virginia: "Hold yourself straight, my little Goat." But "my little

Goat" makes all the difference. What Ramsay wants—minus the way he wants it—is valid; but he has left out certain preparatory steps in striking his heroic pose, and certain truths about himself. First of all, his wife has to keep from him her worries about household finances and other daily problems, and her own adverse feelings about his work, for these are "homely truths" he cannot face without breaking into senseless rages. Secondly, and most importantly, he himself requires emotional reassurance of a childlike order from his wife so as to overcome his sense of failure; and so we get the famous scene in which Mrs. Ramsay becomes "the fountain and spray of life," of "delicious fecundity," into which he plunges his sterile brass male beak, demanding and receiving the sympathy by which his vanity, his "satisfaction in his own splendour," is effectively restored, and becoming then "like a child who"—filled by maternal succor—"drops off satisfied" (*TTL*, pp. 48, 58–60). The satiric line is plain, and for the most part highly effective; but it is not quite adequate to the situation: for we all require some such reassurance, and Ramsay's problem is not that he wants it so badly but that he allows none to others and gives very little, and not very often, in return. Mrs. Ramsay, for her part, gives too often and too much and is slowly sapped of her fecund strength.

Meanwhile her amazing resources, her radiant generosities, are movingly conveyed. She is concerned not only with her son's feelings, his immediate and long-range emotional needs, but with those of the Lighthouse keeper's tubercular son, for whom she is knitting hairy reddish-brown stockings, and for the keeper himself, into whose daily boredom she thinks her way, and for whom she will find "a pile of old magazines, and some tobacco, indeed, whatever she could find lying about":

> For how would you like to be shut up for a whole month at a time, and possibly more in stormy weather, upon a rock the size of a tennis lawn? she would ask; and to have no letters or newspapers, and to see nobody; if you were married not to see your wife, not to know how your children were,—if they were ill, if they had fallen down and broken their legs or arms; to see the same dreary waves breaking week after week, and then a dreadful storm coming, and

the windows covered with spray, and birds dashed against the lamp, and the whole place rocking, and not be able to put your nose out of doors for fear of being swept into the sea? How would you like that? she asked, addressing herself particularly to her daughters. So she added, rather differently, one must take them whatever comforts one can. [*TTL*, pp. 11–12]

At least one of her daughters, given the accents of Julia Stephen at work in this passage, would inherit this uncanny need to imagine oneself into and so recreate in great detail a total human situation, and would transmit her mother's inculcated empathy into verbal description, even as another daughter would transmit it into paint. Consider in this light the telling image from the early memoir, "Reminiscences," of Julia Stephen "standing by the open door of a railway carriage which was taking Stella and some others to Cambridge, and striking out in a phrase or two pictures of all the people who came past her along the platform, and so she kept them laughing till the train went" (*MB*, p. 36). This is, of course, the historic point where the attempt to recreate for us those famous railway passengers, Mrs. Brown of "Mr. Bennett and Mrs. Brown" (1924) and the unfortunate Aunt Minnie of "An Unwritten Novel" (1920), begins. It suggests, rather strongly, I think, that if Leslie Stephen is the obvious source of his daughter's critical and analytic powers, Julia Stephen is the secret source of her creative vision. But what Virginia turned into verbal art, her mother employed for empathetic acts of personal and social concern—a gift which Virginia sometimes mocked but more often envied, and to which she pays her own full empathetic tribute in her portrait of Mrs. Ramsay.

Thus Mrs. Ramsay wants to give to her son, and to the Lighthouse keeper and his son, and to Charles Tansley and the poor woman in town, and to her demanding husband and frightened daughter Cam, the reassurance they need to face life bravely; and we see in each case how sensitively she determines and responds to that universal need. Against her stoic solicitude, moreover, the author places Mr. Ramsay's "Damn you!"—his indecent and obtuse response when she again questions his view of tomorrow's weather: "To pursue truth with such astonishing

lack of consideration for other people's feelings, to rend the thin
veils of civilisation so wantonly, so brutally, was to her so horrible
an outrage of human decency that, without replying, dazed and
blinded, she bent her head as if to let the pelt of jagged hail, the
drench of dirty water, bespatter her unrebuked. There was nothing to be said" (*TTL*, p. 51). To which silent gesture he now
humbly replies that he will step over and ask the Coastguard, if she
likes, about the weather and at once she feels "there is nobody she
reverenced more" and that she is "not good enough to tie his shoe
strings" (*TTL*, p. 51). In this telling moment Virginia Woolf
presents in essence the brutality of her father's rages, as she knew
them in overwhelming fullness after his wife's death, and the
abasement of her mother's reverence for her truth-telling tyrant,
which she had witnessed in childhood. Queen and Tyrant, then,
worshipping at each other's thrones in seesaw fashion: how could
Virginia Woolf accept romantic marriage after that? Yet the
attempt in *To the Lighthouse* is to justify, to celebrate, to com-
mend the love between this well-matched ill-matched pair.

Thus Lily Briscoe, in discussing Mr. Ramsay's shortcom-
ings with her friend William Bankes—his unselfish, generous,
purehearted, wifeless, childless peer and double, a great man of
science and the finest man she knows—still secretly prefers petty,
selfish, vain, tyrannical, failed Mr. Ramsay because of his "fiery
unworldliness," his love of dogs and children, his homage to his
wife's beauty and to the family circle over which she presides
(*TTL*, pp. 40–41); but above all she prefers him for the love he
shares with Mrs. Ramsay, which disarms all criticism of him in its
vital wholeness:

> Directly one looked up and saw them, what she called "being in
> love" flooded them. They became part of that unreal but penetrat-
> ing and exciting universe which is the world seen through the eyes
> of love. The sky stuck to them; the birds sang through them. And,
> what was even more exciting, she felt, too, as she saw Mr. Ramsay
> bearing down and retreating, and Mrs. Ramsay sitting with James
> in the window and the cloud moving and the tree bending, how life,
> from being made up of little separate incidents which one lived one
> by one, became curled and whole like a wave which bore one up

with it and threw one down with it, there, with a dash on the beach. [*TTL*, pp. 72–73]

To be in love, apparently, as the Ramsays are in love, is to be possessed by an intoxicating state which makes life whole, but which is for some reason "unreal." It is a love, moreover, peculiarly framed by the image of "Mrs. Ramsay sitting with James in the window," and it is to this picture that Mr. Bankes responds now with a different kind of rapture, one that disarms all criticism of Mrs. Ramsay:

> For him to gaze as Lily saw him gazing at Mrs. Ramsay was a rapture, equivalent, Lily felt, to the loves of dozens of young men (and perhaps Mrs. Ramsay had never excited the loves of dozens of young men). It was love, she thought, pretending to move her canvas, distilled and filtered; love that never attempted to clutch its object; but, like the love which mathematicians bear their symbols, or poets their phrases, was meant to be spread over the world and become part of the human gain. So it was indeed. The world by all means should have shared it, could Mr. Bankes have said why that woman pleased him so; why the sight of her reading a fairy tale to her boy had upon him precisely the same effect as the solution of a scientific problem, so that he rested in contemplation of it, and felt, as he felt when he had proved something absolute about the digestive system of plants, that barbarity was tamed, the reign of chaos subdued. (*TTL*, pp. 73–74]

A love distilled and filtered, then, and so better than the clutching loves of dozens of young men; a contemplative love, apparently, of late-Victorian madonna and child, the absolute beauty of the maternal bond, without which life could not begin. Such is the rapture Mrs. Ramsay rouses in the hearts of admiring men; and in Lily's heart too, for Mr. Bankes has just given her the aesthetic rationale for her modern abstract painting of James and Mrs. Ramsay in the window. Fair enough. But what are we to make of the clutching love which precedes it and makes life whole? That too is a mother and child relation, only between adults, one of whom is a fractious child soothed by maternal solicitude. Or is it only when Ramsay too feels this abstract rapture for the maternal bond, its absolute beauty, upon which he bears down threateningly and then retreats, that life is made whole? That seems to be the case, and Mrs. Ramsay's reciprocal reverence for his "splendid mind," his professional "greatness," his worldly reputation, seems to be its pale complement, much undercut by satiric references to stoppage at the letter *R*.

Or is it quite the case? Isn't it rather an intimacy, a closeness, which Lily Briscoe wants for herself—a living maternal bond and dependency upon which *this* family circle rests, its Victorian ambience here updated to the years before World War I? Mrs. Ramsay seems to invoke some such closeness when she admits that marriage, which she pushes upon all her young friends, "needed—oh, all sorts of qualities . . . one—she need not name it—that was essential; the thing she had with her husband" (*TTL*, p. 93). So the abstract rapture depends upon this living bond, this living and immediate "thing," which Virginia Woolf finds exciting and unifying, but again, as in *Mrs. Dalloway*, in some sense "unreal."[4]

Meaning, perhaps, that there are things missing from any such blissful picture which undercut its truth, or that she doesn't wholly understand such bliss, or can't rely on it—can't bring it off as her mother did in different times—and therefore questions its validity. Let us assume all three possibilities as we look at what she makes and fails to make of it.

Mrs. Ramsay herself makes the standard criticism of her queenly role: "that all this desire of hers to give, to help, was vanity . . . that she wished so instinctively to help, to give, that people might say of her, 'O Mrs. Ramsay! dear Mrs. Ramsay . . .' and need her and send for her and admire her" (*TTL*, p.69). She recalls, moreover, charges made against her by other parents, of robbing them of their children's affections, of "wishing to dominate, wishing to interfere" and control—as with her present effective attempt to bring Paul Rayley and Minta Doyle together in a marriage which soon fares badly. And Lily too observes the self-serving fallibility of her pity for men like Bankes and Carmichael, who are secure in themselves and their work and need no pity.

She is vain and manipulative, then, at her worst, in carrying out her queenly role. Her jealousy of Minta once the engagement she has maneuvered has taken place and her husband has responded gallantly to the young girl's "golden haze," her awareness of his preference for "these golden-reddish girls, with something . . . a little wild and harum-scarum about them . . . some quality which she herself had not" (*TTL*, pp.148–49), suggests further a vicarious involvement in the marriages she urges, as if she sought thereby some missing component in her own marriage to the otherwise dried-up Ramsay. Does she then dominate and manipulate him so he will need and admire her, and perhaps also withhold something from him in revenge for his own withholdings?

There is much evidence in the text, and in the lives behind the text, which supports these points. Consider first the traces of Julia Stephen's first marriage to Herbert Duckworth. Early in the novel, when Mrs. Ramsay hears that the Swiss maid's father is dying of cancer (as would Leslie Stephen at seventy-two) and responds with that characteristic sadness that so enhances her beauty, there is a speculative passage following the repeated refrain, "Never did anybody look so sad":

> But was it nothing but looks, people said? What was there behind it—her beauty and splendour? Had he blown his brains out, they asked, had he died the week before they were [to be] married—some other, earlier lover, of whom rumours reached one? Or was there nothing? nothing but an incomparable beauty which she lived behind, and could do nothing to disturb? For easily though she might have said at some moment of intimacy when stories of great passion, of love foiled, or ambition thwarted came her way how she too had known or felt or been through it herself, she never spoke. She was silent always. She knew then—she knew without having learnt. Her simplicity fathomed what clever people falsified. Her singleness of mind made her drop plumb like a stone, alight exact as a bird, gave her, naturally, this swoop and fall of the spirit upon truth which delighted, eased, sustained—falsely perhaps. [*TTL*, p. 46]

The last thought probably refers to her ability to hit upon delightful assuagements of terror or despair, by which a boar's skull becomes a bird's nest or mountain landscape, as that bird

simile suggests. But it also draws away, oddly, from her prob-
lematic sadness; and its temporizing "falsely perhaps" obscures
the fact that an attribution of pure intuitive simplicity makes this
"blue madonna streaked with tears" an almost incredible person,
at least in this one regard. She is a great deal more wonderful, for
instance, than Julia Duckworth, who like most mortals learned
the hard way about life's harshness when, in the fourth year of
their marriage, her first husband suddenly died and she was left to
raise three children by herself. Her stoic outlook and ingrained
melancholy *followed* from that event, as did whatever intuitive
simplicities she then avidly applied to the misfortunes of others.
Interestingly, having had this experience, she too never spoke
about it, at least to her highly curious children by two marriages,
who between them developed their own romantic family legend
about it, as we have seen, of perfect and complete happiness and
shattering loss—and, in Virginia's case, of ghostly reunion after
her mother's death, so oddly reflected by the grammatical slip
above ("had he died the week before they were married . . .?") by
which the rumored "earlier love" becomes a ghostly husband.

Is Mrs. Ramsay's borrowed silence a cover-up, then, for
missing widowhood and continuing ghostly union? Unlike Julia
Stephen, she apparently has nothing to tell. Yet she is also silent or
evasive when she *does* have things to tell, as when her husband
wants her to share her ingrained sadness and she calls it "wool-
gathering" (though, interestingly, at the precise moment he notes
her sadness, she conceives her eternal oneness with surrounding
life as that of "a bride" rising like a mist "to meet her lover" [*TTL*,
pp. 97–98, 104]);or when he wants her to tell him that she loves
him and she acknowledges instead his rightness about the weather
(*TTL*, p. 184). The long first section, "The Window," ends in fact
with her "triumph" over him in again not saying in so many
words that she loves him, though he knows from her radiant smile
and consummate happiness that she does.

Well, yes, of course she loves him, but triumphing over him
is also necessary to her love; and though it is supposed to imply the
triumph of unspoken communication, of selfless inner being, over
the inadequacies of words and the vanities of mere personalities, it
may mean something else as well: namely, that she *doesn't* love

him passionately, as Julia Duckworth loved Herbert, and so *can't* tell him she loves him in so many words. Suppose we posit here that her spoken vows belong to another man, a ghostly thief of love who exists, or once existed, outside the text, but whom Virginia Woolf is now trying (not always successfully) to suppress. This would explain Mrs. Ramsay's curious silences, and it would also explain why she is so remote from Ramsay, in her melancholia, that he cannot "protect her." After all, what intuitive "simplicity" makes her behave in these remote and silent ways— she who has so many reassuring words for other sufferers and, indeed, for all his other sufferings? Is it really because "he could say things" whereas "she never could say what she felt," as Virginia Woolf asserts (*TTL*, p. 185)?

In a recent review of Leslie Stephen's *Mausoleum Book* Francis Wyndham makes the nice point that Julia Stephen remained "a kind of widow" even through her second marriage, "serenely moving in a higher sphere where the consciousness of tragedy was never far from the surface."[5] It was a sphere so high, apparently, that Leslie Stephen, like Mr. Ramsay, could never reach her. He too wanted to break into her sorrow—wanted her to say to him in so many words, I love you—and had to settle for loving her reticence when she did not. No wonder that Virginia Stephen fantasized for her reticent mother a dead clergyman husband whom she longed for, and hallucinated his return as that mysterious man sitting on the edge of her bed when she died, as if filling out the family script! But for Mrs. Ramsay she could not bring herself to imagine, much less hallucinate, that missing widowhood which explains her silent, remote, and melancholy ways, nor that romantic first marriage which explains her withholdings and her apparent need to keep Ramsay hanging and unsatisfied, as he obviously kept her long unsatisfied, whatever their domestic bliss. A de facto widow, she has settled for maternal control over her dependent childlike husband, and has encouraged his dependency, in the absence of, among other things, that "great passion," sexual as well as affectionate, which she might have enjoyed with a different husband.

In the text itself the absence of such passion between the Ramsays is hinted at in several ways. The most obvious confirmation comes when Ramsay retires to his study after dinner, still smarting from a rebuff to Scott's fiction which implies that his own work might not last, and finds in Scott's handling of "poor Steenie's drowning and Mucklebackit's sorrow" in *The Antiquary* evidence not only of his lasting value but of his superiority as well to French novelists in their concern with sexual love (*TTL* p. 180). Invigorated and moved to tears by Scott's example, Ramsay uses the word *fiddlesticks* to define the French concern; and watching his wife reading Shakespeare's sonnets beside him, he further concludes that "the whole of life did not consist in going to bed with a woman" (*TTL*, p. 181). In weeping over death and dismissing sex he is, of course, very much like his Clapham forebears, as A.O.J. Cockshut argues;[6] but the comfort he takes here for his own professional failure may also reflect another kind of failure. Mrs. Ramsay intimates as much while dressing for dinner, and seeing outside the window a sight which always amuses her, "the rooks trying to decide which tree to settle on," and the old father rook with half his wing feathers missing, "a bird of a very trying and difficult disposition" whom she calls "old Joseph" (and whom we may as well call "old Ramsay"), fighting with another rook: " 'Look!' she said, laughing. They were actually fighting, Joseph and Mary were fighting. Anyhow they all went up again, and the air was shoved aside by their black wings and cut into exquisite scimitar shapes" (*TTL*, pp. 121–22). If this parable on her own marriage makes her laugh, and its outcome seems to her lovely, and if she tries now to keep her son Jasper from shooting at such pathetic personified birds, those "scimitar shapes" remind us all the same of that sterile beak of brass, "the arid scimitar of the male," which plunges into her "fountain and spray of life" in earlier pages, demanding sympathy. Of course, all males seem sterile to Mrs. Ramsay, and in need of her protection; but the Joseph and Mary story goes beyond sterility to suggest displacement by some more potent spirit—such as Herbert Duckworth. [7]

Mrs. Ramsay's recollection of Carrie and Herbert Manning in her dinner conversation with William Bankes, who has received a letter from Carrie, may yield still another trace of that more potent spirit: for the Mannings were a couple she had known briefly twenty years back (the time, relatively, of Julia Stephen's first marriage) who did things decisively, stuck to plans when they made them, slayed pesky dragons ("Never should she forget Herbert killing a wasp with a teaspoon on the bank"), and lived in a "dream land" of the past, in their house on the Thames, where life lay "like a lake, placidly between the banks," and where she moved "without haste or anxiety; for there was no future to worry about." Now, as she converses about them with Bankes, she moves about "like a ghost" on that day "very still and beautiful" when she first visited them (*TTL*, pp.132, 140). But she hasn't thought about them for years, and it is probably too much to find in this preserved idyll more than a few traces—a suggestively virile name and manner, a protected carefree life—of that missing first marriage. We may want to place more emphasis instead on the tale of the fisherman and his wife Mrs. Ramsay reads that day to her son James, the fairy tale that figures so importantly in everybody's vision of the Ramsays' love: "She read on: 'Ah wife,' said the man, 'why should we be King? I do not want to be King.' 'Well,' said the wife, 'if you won't be King, I will; go to the Flounder, for I will be King' " (*TTL*, p. 86).

Somewhere between the first and third sections of the novel Mr. Ramsay, a decided flounderer in kingly matters himself, seems to have gone to the Flounder for advice about his wife's request; for in taking the children to the Lighthouse he belatedly acknowledges her Kingship, involving not merely her supremacy in love but also her rightness about the primacy of kindness over truth. It is his kind of mission, moreover: an heroic expedition, most of which he spends with his head buried in a book, to deliver the brown parcels she had planned to send to the keeper and his son ten years before. On the journey Ramsay is said to "escape" into his book, which becomes an expedition in thought, a scramble up mental mountains. But books and poems have other functions for him, and the question of what he is doing inside them is crucial to his character.

"Someone had blundered" is the refrain he repeats aloud through the first section of the novel, embarrassing his wife and his guests by the intensity of his involvement with the poem's futile heroics. In Tennyson's "Charge of the Light Brigade," itself a prime example of the pointless heroic posturing of an age unsure of its values, Mr. Ramsay finds a moving instance of his own self-dramatizing pity, his own pointlessly heroic blunders as a failed philosopher. And he is ridiculously lovable, if embarrassing, in being forced to seek emotional comfort in this manner. His Victorian posturing takes a more mellow form as both he and Augustus Carmichael recite Charles Elton's "Luriana, Lurilee" at the end of dinner (*TTL*, pp. 166–67), and so acknowledge his wife's unifying social powers, her dinner-table artistry, which in its creation of a human stay against chaotic night partakes (we are told) "of eternity" (*TTL*, p. 158).

On the voyage to the Lighthouse the refrain which possesses him, and which his children echo in turn as they come to side with him, is "we perished, each alone," from Cowper's "The Castaway." He has been living inside this poem, apparently, since his wife's death, and—if at seventy-one he has, like Leslie Stephen, only a year more to live—in anticipation of his own. In his excitement he repeats the lines aloud, to his children's outrage, and then murmurs gently the self-pitying lines: "But I beneath a rougher sea / Was whelmed in deeper gulfs than he." Taking "he" as his wife we may indeed ponder his continuing vanity; but if the "he" is also Herbert Duckworth, in its biographical ambiguities, he has his point. He has lived longer and more dependently with the same woman, has now outlived her rather than died before her, and is more lost without her than she would be without him—or than her prototype was without Herbert Duckworth. But if his extremes of grief and vanity reflect his continuing dependency, he has nonetheless converted, in his remoteness, his gloom, his dignity, and now in his symbolic act of compassion, to her side. We learn of his tyranny in his widower years from his children, but all we see of it is their forced obedience now in joining his Lighthouse mission. We learn of his insatiable demands for sympathy in his grief from women, and of his delight in receiving it: but when, with histrionic groans and sighs, he demands such sympathy now from Lily Briscoe, and she finally manages to compliment his boots, he is released by her comic tribute to male vanity to a new and final phase "when it seemed as if he had shed worries and ambitions, and the hope of sympathy and the desire for praise, had entered some other region, was drawn up, as if by curiosity, in dumb colloquy, whether with himself or another [Mrs. Ramsay?], at the head of that little procession out of one's range" (*TTL*, p. 233). So Lily last sees him, this man who in her previous angry judgment "never gave," always "took" (*TTL*, p. 223). But he has just given her a lesson in tying knots, in return for her compliment, and has moved her thereby to tears of sympathy which will help her to untie the mental knot that binds her painter's mind. And on the voyage to the Lighthouse he gives to his daughter Cam sufficient sympathy to remind her of those library moments "when he was not vain, nor a tyrant, and did not wish you to pity him," and was likely to ask "as gently as any one could, Was there nothing he could give her?" (*TTL*, p. 282). And to his son James, who still wants to kill him for childhood tyrannies, for brutal sarcasms and intolerable vanities now recalled, he gives the expeditionary kudos, "Well done!" and so includes him in his own stern vision of stoic manhood (*TTL*, p. 306). And to them he seems himself a "young man" again, brave and upright in a godless world—a young man for whom they will "do anything" as he springs from the boat to the Lighthouse rock (*TTL*, p. 308).

This was how Virginia Woolf saw her father in his final days, when it seemed to her a new and better phase of his life was just beginning. Cam and James at seventeen and sixteen, like Virginia and Adrian at twenty-two and twenty-one, are old enough to begin to be possible companions to their father; and there is fit lightheartedness in this final tribute to his better fictive self. But the spirit which moves him, and which makes him accessible to his children, is that of his wife, whose belief in the need for reassurance in a godless world he now quixotically expedites and (all too faintly) mimes, and so reunites the family he has ravaged, more savagely in life than in this fiction, and for them at least unites her wisdom with his own ability to reach the letter *R*.

This was as close as Virginia Woolf would ever come to imagining a man strong enough to match her mother's emotionally creative powers and to restore her own shaky belief in romantic marriage. She knew, from the intense mothering she received from Leonard Woolf for the better part of her career, that men are not by definition emotionally sterile, that they too may provide nurturing love: but she never acknowledged this in her fiction—never showed a woman depending as heavily as she did upon Leonard for the strength and reassurance to go on being creative, being herself. The demands she made upon his sympathies were more terrible, if more real, than those her father made upon his wife and daughters. Her fear of failure in her writings, her preoccupation with literary fame, was more devastating in its consequences for Leonard and herself, in terms of actual illness, than her father's all too exemplary fears in their immediate consequences for his wife and family: but of course it is his egotism she repeats and dislikes in herself—and castigates in him. Her "madness" was her excuse for faults very like his own, to which she never really admitted, perhaps because of her own concern with "greatness," in which—to be sure—her husband shared.

She was right, however, to look to her mother's life for some insight into her own creative powers and possibilities, for she owed most of her creative strengths—her intuitive, empathetic, and poetic powers, her impressive private reaches, her easy sociabilities—to this remarkable woman. But she could not look to her mother's death in this novel, nor even in *The Years*, without being overwhelmed in that deeper gulf of self-dramatizing pity her father so foolishly claimed for himself, hence she wisely avoided it. This meant, however, that she had to borrow Lily Briscoe's grief from her own buried fund of confused childhood feelings, minus her own psychic history, even as she had borrowed Mrs. Ramsay's silences from Julia Stephen's absent widowhood.

The "Time Passes" section of the novel is itself the prime reflection in Virgina Woolf's fiction of her initial inability to grieve her mother's death, and of the long delay in releasing her unspent emotions. Instead of facing up in this section to the impact of Mrs. Ramsay's death upon her husband and children, she devotes it to the question of her continuing spiritual presence and leaves her death for the family friend, Lily Briscoe, to cope with ten years later. Lily's position in this regard is very much like her own in writing the novel; but then the evasiveness of the "Time Passes" section is also very much her own evasiveness in breaking with "the unity of [her] design." Her nominal intention is to show, through the passage of time, the randomness of senseless death and the persistence beyond it of certain imperishable human qualities. Her choice of the summer home at Skye is in this regard like her choice of Jacob's room, in the novel of that title, as a register of human presence. As such it runs counter to her objections to Arnold Bennett's fiction, whose environmental detail was supposedly inadequate as an index to human character; but then she works the environment for unusual spiritual evidence, almost for mystic meaning.

    Narrating the section through the common selfless voice she had developed in *Mrs. Dalloway*, she personifies the forces of change and disintegration as "the little airs," detached from the rougher wind outside, which press through the deserted house asking assorted domestic objects how long they will endure. The allegorical device is, to say the least, precious and pretentious, not because "airs" are unsuitable to a decaying summer house as agents of disintegrative inquiry, but because the level of inquiry is too safely abstruse to yield much anguished meaning. Walt Disney's animated cartoons often do as well or better with such devices, though for less serious ends. We learn nonetheless that the bedrooms of the house stand fast against the first inroads of decay, if only because there are still living sleepers inside them. It is the last night of the summer occupancy, after which the "stray airs, advance guards of great armies," may come in and do their work without human resistance. But even then the loveliness and stillness observed by common selfless consciousness remain steadfast in the bedroom, clasping ethereal hands, as evidence that the spirit of Mrs. Ramsay still persists. Meanwhile "divine goodness," also personified, is foiled by the force of destruction; anonymous sleepless beach-walkers are unable to get answers from the sea and the night as to the whys and wherefores of existence; and the death of Mrs. Ramsay is recorded in a brief parenthesis: "(Mr. Ramsay, stumbling along a passage one dark morning, stretched his arms out, but Mrs. Ramsay having died rather suddenly the night before, his arms, though stretched out, remained empty)" (*TTL*, p. 194). We know that Virginia Stephen offered to fill such arms on the actual occasion of her mother's death, when her father charged past her without noticing her need to share their common grief. She may well be avenging herself here, but death's ironic triumph is all we witness.

Shortly after this the seventy-year-old cleaning woman, Mrs. McNab, arrives to sing her witless caretaking song of human persistency, and we get one of those painfully inauthentic attempts, like that of the beggar woman in the park in *Mrs. Dalloway*, to show the historic sweep of human suffering through the lyric sensibility of a proletarian woman. Then the deaths of Prue and Andrew Ramsay are parenthetically recorded—hers (like Stella Duckworth's) from "some illness connected with childbirth" (*TTL*, p. 199); his (like Jacob Flanders's) by an exploding shell in France in World War I (*TTL*, p. 201); and the narrative view expands to include "gigantic chaos" outside the house and "idiot games" (recalling the "idiot boy" in Kensington Gardens) in a universe "battling and tumbling, in brute confusion and wanton lust aimlessly by itself" (*TTL*, pp. 202–3). Against these odds the heroic Mrs. McNab invokes her sisterly memory of Mrs. Ramsay coming up the drive with the washing, calling out to the servants, stooping over her flowers, then dissolving into a yellow-beamed lady in a gray cloak (recalling that womblike "film of semi-transparent yellow" through which the author peered in childhood) wandering over the walls and furniture with her as she works. The Lighthouse beam, with which Mrs. Ramsay had identified in one of her selfless and eternal moments of private wedge-shaped being while she lived, underscores her persisting presence; and so inspirited, the forces of human persistency prevail as Mrs. McNab, joined by Mrs. Bast and her son George, begin to restore the house to its former habitableness, in preparation for the approaching expeditionary hero, Mr. Ramsay, four of his six remaining children, the belated mourner Lily Briscoe, and other friends. By these worked-up allegorical devices, then, the impersonal narrator sweeps over the actual impact of Julia Stephen's death, the funereal gloom, tyranny, and outrage which enveloped her survivors, and the whole question of unworked grief from which, we know, the need to write this novel arose. If sentimentality is, as I. A. Richards holds, a form of inhibition, the middle section is decidedly sentimental.

The question of unworked grief is left, of course, for Lily Briscoe to solve in the final section. But why she should grieve Mrs. Ramsay at all, or be so involved with her in life as to feel such want, pain, and anger at her death, we do not know. Nor does the concluding section ever explain it. Still, in memorable and moving fashion, it records the emotions and confusions which Virginia Woolf herself must have undergone at the time of her mother's death, and the process of therapeutic release she underwent, along with Lily, in creating this objective correlative for grieving. Thus Lily, like Virginia at her mother's deathbed and for thirty years thereafter, feels "nothing, nothing—nothing that she could express at all" on coming back "after all these years and Mrs. Ramsay dead" (*TTL*, p. 217). Alone at the breakfast table, she again wonders why she has come, for the thought of "Mrs. Ramsay dead; Andrew killed; Prue dead too—repeat it as she might, . . . roused no feeling in her" (*TTL*, p. 219). She is also angry with Mrs. Ramsay for dying and leaving her to cope with Mr. Ramsay's oppressive demands for sympathy, which prevent her from redoing her unfinished painting of ten years past. The incommensurate nature of her anger is instructive; her reaction to Mr. Ramsay in the crucial passage below, and to Mrs. Ramsay as its secret departed cause, is that of a child raised by colossal parents rather than a friend on a weekend stay at a summer house. As such it is plainly borrowed from the author's life and smuggled into this forty-four-year-old spinster's midlife crisis, her wasting time and talent, which for no evident reason she also blames on Mrs. Ramsay:

> That man, she thought, her anger rising in her, never gave; that man took. She, on the other hand, would be forced to give. Mrs. Ramsay had given. Giving, giving, giving, she had died—and had left all this. Really, she was angry with Mrs. Ramsay. With the brush slightly trembling in her fingers she looked to the hedge, the step, the wall. Here was Lily, at forty-four, unable to do a thing, standing there, playing at painting, playing at the one thing one did not play at, and it was all Mrs. Ramsay's fault. She was dead. The step where she used to sit was empty. She was dead.
> But why repeat this over and over again? Why be always

trying to bring up some feeling she had not got? There was a kind of blasphemy in it. It was all dry; all withered; all spent. [*TTL*, pp. 223–24]

Why indeed does Lily feel this terrible repeated need to bring up some long-blocked feeling about Mrs. Ramsay's death? The text never tells us; the life-sources of her unworked grief are all we have to go by—the image from the late memoir, for instance, of Virginia Stephen, aged thirteen, stretching out her arms to a father who never gave, on that early morning when a mother who gave too much had stopped giving altogether and had left her to cope with life's confusions. Her anger with her mother for leaving her, implicit then in her inability to grieve, is filtered now through this spinster surrogate whose childlike attachment to the Ramsays is so oddly and inexplicably a textual given. One brief notation, that she is a spinster who keeps house for her father off the Brompton Road (*TTL*, p. 32), allows us to *deduce* the rationale for her attachment already mentioned: for she has obviously lost her mother at some unspecified age, and—perhaps through Mrs. Ramsay's ready solicitude—has since felt the need to adopt this family for her own, and through them to work out the terms of her own parental relations. We are told nothing helpful, however, about her previous relations with the Ramsays, and *nothing at all* about her actual parents: but from Virginia Woolf's parental relations we can understand why Lily now wants to be like Mrs. Ramsay, to be able to give sympathy to her husband in the late-Victorian manner, why she rebukes now her own sexual unworthiness in refusing that traditional woman's role and concludes that she is "not a woman, but a peevish, ill-tempered, dried-up old maid" (*TTL*, p. 226). For she is facing now the problem which Virginia Stephen faced at thirteen with her mother's death, and again at fifteen with Stella Duckworth's death—how to become a woman without maternal guidance. As her adopted mother, Mrs. Ramsay had disparaged Lily's art and had tried to marry her off to William Bankes; but she had also admired Lily's defiant spirit as akin to her own silent inner strength, and without intending it, she had created for her a model of sympathetic artistry in life which, after her death, gives life to

Lily's art. Thus Lily, an emotionally undeveloped woman, must not only come to terms with Mrs. Ramsay before she can finish her painting, she must also emulate her creativity in life, in marriage, at every step of her artistic work. Her artistry is in fact a maternal inheritance, a distilled result of maternal guidance long-delayed by death and emotional arrest, and even her spinsterhood is a distillation of Mrs. Ramsay's marital withholdings. She is in these regards rather like Stephen Dedalus, another remorseful griever, whose sterile artistry must be fertilized by his relations with "adopted" parents. But more to the point, Lily at forty-four, divided between life and art, is like Virginia Woolf in her forties as she writes this novel, trying to convert her ungrieved grief into a lasting portrait of the lost beloved:

> For how could one express in words these emotions of the body? express that emptiness there? (She was looking at the drawing-room steps: they looked extraordinarily empty.) It was one's body feeling, not one's mind. The physical sensations that went with that bare look of the steps had become suddenly extremely unpleasant. To want and not to have, sent all up her body a hardness, a hollowness, a strain. And then to want and not to have—to want and want—how that wrung the heart, and wrung it again and again! Oh, Mrs. Ramsay! she called out silently, to that essence which sat by the boat, that abstract one made of her, that woman in grey, as if to abuse her for having gone, and then having gone, come back again. It had seemed so safe, thinking of her. Ghost, air, nothingness, a thing you could play with easily and safely at any time of day or night, she had been that, and then suddenly she put her hand out and wrung the heart thus. [*TTL*, pp. 265–66]

Lily's heart is wrung, apparently, by the grief which Virginia Stephen had failed to release when her mother died, by her anger at being deserted by the woman she loved and wanted so much,[8] and by the return of that repressed anger and its beloved ghostly object. Thus Lily's eyes now fill with tears, as she tries to look at her painting, and she cries for Mrs. Ramsay "without being aware of any unhappiness" (*TTL*, p. 268). Then, calling in imagination to old Mr. Carmichael on the lawn beside her, she begins asking questions about such unexpected and miraculous events, and she feels "that if they both got up, here, now on the lawn, and demanded an explanation" of life as to its shortness and inexplicability, "then beauty would roll itself up; the space would fill; those empty flourishes would form into shape; if they shouted loud enough Mrs. Ramsay would return. 'Mrs. Ramsay!' she said aloud, 'Mrs. Ramsay!' The tears ran down her face" (*TTL*, p. 268). When Mrs. Ramsay fails to come, Lily is ashamed of her ignominious cry of pain and want and "bitter anger"; but gradually the pain subsides and, with "a relief that was balm in itself," she senses Mrs. Ramsay's presence by her side, then sees her moving off in all her beauty, "raising to her forehead a wreath of white flowers with which she went":

> Lily squeezed her tubes again. She attacked that problem of the hedge. It was strange how clearly she saw her, stepping with her usual quickness across fields among whose folds, purplish and soft, among whose flowers, hyacinth or lilies, she vanished. It was some trick of the painter's eye. For days after she had heard of her death she had seen her thus, putting her wreath to her forehead *and going unquestioningly with her companion, a shade across the fields*. The sight, the phrase, had its power to console. Wherever she happened to be, painting, here, in the country or in London, the vision would come to her, and her eyes, half closing, sought something to base her vision on. She looked down the railway carriage, the omnibus; took a line from shoulder or cheek; looked at the windows opposite, at Piccadilly, lamp-strung in the evening. All had been part of the fields of death. [*TTL*, pp. 269–70; italics mine]

Virginia Woolf's first memories were of riding with her mother on train and bus going to Cornwall; and on her mother's death she had even hallucinated that man sitting on the edge of her mother's bed whom I am going to propose now as the otherwise unidentified companion with whom Mrs. Ramsay goes so unquestioningly, "a shade across the fields." We may want to call the companion Death rather than Herbert Duckworth; but I think the edge lies rather with some waiting ghostly person, as it did when her mother died, and that the consolation lies in Stella Duckworth's prescient response to that hallucination: "It's nice that she shouldn't be alone" (*MB*, p. 92). Certainly the *two* companions Lily later imagines with Mrs. Ramsay, when she groups her death with those of Prue and Andrew, are ghostly persons; but even here, as the three shades move together across the fields, Mrs. Ramsay walks "rather fast in front, as if she expected to meet some one round the corner" (TTL, p. 299)—no doubt her previous companion of the fields, our fictive prototype for the ghost of Herbert Duckworth, that first and most beloved husband of Julia Stephen. That she walked so in life (as Woolf notes on pp. 19–20) suggests that she has always been on the lookout for such deathly companions, or for her impending deathly reunion with at least one who had gone before her.[9]

It is at this point, when Lily has grouped her dead in what seems to be her psychological version of the Elysian Fields, that someone sits in the drawing-room chair where Mrs. Ramsay had first posed for her painting, and settles "by some stroke of luck so as to throw an odd-shaped triangular shadow over the step." With this symbol of private wedge-shaped selfless being reestablished, Mrs. Ramsay again comes back to her. At first the old horror—"to want and want and not to have"—comes back too; but when Mrs. Ramsay seems to refrain from inflicting it, it becomes "part of ordinary experience," and Lily moves to the edge of the lawn to share her vision of Mrs. Ramsay in her "perfect goodness," knitting the reddish-brown stocking for the Lighthouse keeper's boy, with Mr. Ramsay, whom she now "wants" for the first time. And in this state of resolved emotion she is able to finish her painting.

What does it mean when Lily says of Mr. Ramsay now, "She wanted him" (TTL, p. 300)? Will the forty-four-year-old spinster marry the seventy-one-year-old widower? That seems unlikely, though Mrs. Ramsay had once intended her for Ramsay's contemporary, William Bankes. The more probable meaning is that she is now sufficiently one with Mrs. Ramsay to be able to give him freely the womanly sympathy he needs; and in fact, as she surmises that he has reached the Lighthouse, she feels that "whatever she had wanted to give him, when he left her that morning, she had given him at last" (TTL, pp. 308–9). It is an odd conclusion, since he is not there to benefit from her changed condition, her newfound "wanting" for him; but perhaps she has beamed it over to him, mystically, or perhaps, in becoming capable of supportive sympathy, she has become the kind of woman Ramsay would approve, and in that sense has conceded to him what she could never before concede. In either case she has become the Ramsays' common heir, a surrogate daughter capable of grieving her mother and comforting her father, and of loving them both selflessly, without clutching demands.

A lovely heritage, then, however long-delayed. Not many of us are able to come to such gratifying terms with our departed or departing parents. But, as Lily's borrowings from the author's life attest, there is something missing in her artistic vision of parental love and daughterly devotion. Ideally she would be released now from spinsterhood, or at least from her skeptical view of the Ramsays' marriage. And she does arrive at a vision of their engagement which *seems* to be her touchstone for romantic love. Thus, late in the novel, remembering how Ramsay would stop dead in front of his wife and "some curious shock" would pass through her (*TTL*, p. 294), she converts the scene into an instance of romantic vowing:

> He stretched out his hand and raised her from the chair. It seemed somehow as if he had once bent in the same way and raised her from a boat which, lying a few inches off some island, had required that the ladies should thus be helped on shore by the gentlemen. An old-fashioned scene that was, which required, very nearly, crinolines and peg-top trousers. Letting herself be helped by him, Mrs. Ramsay had thought (Lily supposed) the time has come now. Yes, she would say it now. Yes, she would marry him. And she stepped slowly, quietly on shore. Probably she said one word only, letting her hand rest still in his; but no more. Time after time the same thrill had passed between them—obviously it had, Lily thought. . . . She was not inventing; she was only trying to smooth out something she had been given years ago folded up; something she had seen. [*TTL*, p. 295]

If Lily is not inventing, Virginia is. As she knew from her father's *Mausoleum Book*, her mother had agreed to marry him while seated in an armchair by her own fireplace one January evening in 1878; she had done so in seventeen measured words, not one, and only after lengthy verbal vacillations recorded in a year's exchange of letters. The crinolines and peg-top trousers came, moreover, from those summers at Little Holland House in her youth—the "summer afternoon world" of eminent men and ladies over which Virginia rhapsodizes in her memoirs (*MB*, pp. 86–87)—when her mother had not yet met Stephen (who had found the place too "alarming" for his taste when he glimpsed her there in 1866!); and the boating metaphor no doubt derived from the tour of Venice and/or Lake Lucerne that summer where her mother first met (and shortly after married) Herbert Duckworth.[10] In other words, Virginia Woolf has transposed the charged romantic ambience of her mother's first engagement to her second, as if finally restoring stolen love! She has restored the missing depth of passion, as signaled by electric vowing, but whether she has done so by sure creative instinct, or by sleight of hand, seems so uncertain that she questions it herself.

Thus Lily moves immediately from this "folded" and decidedly suspect memory to the Ramsays' quarrels—the bedroom door slamming, Mr. Ramsay whizzing a plate through the window—tempests which, though soon resolved in garden colloquies, have taken their emotional toll on Mrs. Ramsay. A bit earlier, moveover, she types such occasions as instances of Mrs. Ramsay's weakness with her husband, for "she let him make those scenes" (*TTL*, p. 291). The problem relates back to her own reluctance to sympathize with this man who never gave, only took. Still, as his token giving on the Lighthouse journey attests, he seems to have learned something about reciprocity since his wife's death, and to that extent the novel defines the possibility, at least, of mutually supportive, if not electric, love. This much, we may hazard, Virginia Woolf herself was able to achieve in her companionate marriage with Leonard Woolf as part of her own parental heritage. But the problem also relates back to Lily's antipathy toward the sexual aspects of marriage as signaled by those electric thrills. In the opening section of the novel she too had been possessed by "the vibration of love" between Paul Rayley and Minta Doyle, so much so that when Paul announced his intention to get up early in the morning to search the beach for Minta's missing brooch, Lily wanted to join him:

Lily wanted to protest violently and outrageously her desire to help him, envisaging how in the dawn on the beach she would be the one to pounce on the brooch half-hidden by some stone, and thus herself be included among the sailors and adventurers. But what did he reply to her offer? She actually said with an emotion that she seldom let appear, "Let me come with you," and he laughed. He meant yes or no—either perhaps. But it was not his meaning—it was the odd chuckle he gave, as if he had said, Throw yourself over the cliff if you like, I don't care. He turned on her cheek the heat of love, its horror, its cruelty, its unscrupulosity. It scorched her, and Lily, looking at Minta, being charming to Mr. Ramsay at the other end of the table, flinched for her exposed to these fangs, and was thankful. For at any rate, she said to herself, catching sight of the salt cellar on the pattern, she need not marry, thank Heaven: she need not undergo that degradation. She was saved from that dilution. She would move the tree rather more to the middle. [*TTL*, pp. 153–54]

Taking this with the undiluted grain of salt provided above, as the sour-grapes response of a spinster who finds compensation in her painting, the difficulty it raises for romantic marriage is nonetheless considerable. For, as Lily now concludes, the love between Paul and Minta—"so beautiful and exciting" that she trembles "on the verge of it" and offers to look for the missing brooch—is also "the stupidest, most barbaric of human passions, and turns a nice young man with a profile like a gem's (Paul's was exquisite) into a bully with a crowbar, (he was swaggering, he was insolent) in the Mile End Road" (*TTL*, p. 154). And she further finds it "tedious, puerile, and inhumane," though also "beautiful and necessary" (*TTL*, p. 155). Having arrived at this internal impasse, she is willing to wait for any further "light upon the question of love" that conversation or time may bring; but ten years later, when she thinks again of the Rayleys, it is only to take satisfaction in their marital disharmonies, in her own spinster-hood, and in Mrs. Ramsay's obvious wrongness about them all. Yet at the very moment of her triumph over Mrs. Ramsay, she is again seized by love's barbaric power:

(Suddenly, as suddenly as a star slides in the sky, a reddish light seemed to burn in her mind, covering Paul Rayley, issuing from him. It rose like a fire sent up in token of some celebration by savages on a distant beach. She heard the roar and the crackle. The whole sea for miles around ran red and gold. Some winey smell mixed with it and intoxicated her, for she felt again her own head-long desire to throw herself off the cliff and be drowned looking for a pearl brooch on a beach. And the roar and the crackle repelled her with fear and disgust, as if while she saw its splendour and power she saw too how it fed on the treasure of the house, greedily, disgustingly, and she loathed it. But for a sight, for a glory it sur-passed everything in her experience, and burnt year after year like a signal fire on a desert island at the edge of the sea, and one had only to say "in love" and instantly, as happened now, up rose Paul's fire again. And it sank and she said to herself, laughing, "The Rayleys".) [*TTL*, pp. 261–62]

As the passage makes abundantly clear, Lily has been sexu-ally attracted to Paul Rayley all these years. But by defining "in love" by his sexual powers, she has moved away from her original definition of what "being in love" meant for the Ramsays. Their crinolines and peg-top trousers seem quite civilized by contrast with Paul's barbaric fires, and we are forced to conclude that their romantic marriage is in some sense asexual, for all the thrills and shocks which occur when their eyes and hands meet; or perhaps more fairly, that their sexuality has been channeled into borrowed gallantries and real quarrels, that compassion is their ruling mode, and that there are no depths of passion between them.

Are we supposed to choose then between marriages of passion and compassion? Not, surely, if they produce bullies of sexuality like Paul Rayley, on the one hand, and bullies of sym-pathy like Mr. Ramsay on the other. Is Mr. Ramsay's belated reciprocity the corrective answer? It makes him young again, but we know already how much he minimizes sexual love. It seems to me, rather, that Lily is confused, that she can deal with sexual attraction between the Rayleys, but not between the Ramsays, because she shares in the author's inability to confront this aspect of her parents' marriage. We have already seen how Virginia Woolf suppresses Mrs. Ramsay's rumored first love, gives to Minta that "harum-scarum" wildness Mrs. Ramsay supposedly lacks, and denies Mrs. Ramsay the clutching admiration of dozens of young men—though in fact her mother was much sought after in her youth (*QB* 1:17) and seems to have had a passionate first marriage. In Lily's repulsion from that fire which feeds "on the treasure of the house," then, we see the author's repulsion from the grievous effects of sexuality on her treasured mother, who left her, as it were, to rejoin her sexually attractive first husband in the fields of death. But this means that the boating metaphor for the Ramsays' romantic union is suspect, that the vital wholeness between them, the unifying wave of life which joins them, is indeed imperfectly understood, and that there is after all something sentimental and "unreal" about their depiction, something confused, at least, in the author's understanding of what makes for romantic marriage—indeed, something transposed from the Duckworth marriage to the Stephen marriage which doesn't really belong there. But at least she could move into her mother's mind and heart in the compelling first section, and could break through, in the final section, to that moving expression of anger, grief, and love which releases her surrogate to selfless sympathy for parental figures and creative independence for herself. This freed her for a time from her parental ghosts, and released her—not to more deeply romantic marriage with Leonard Woolf—but to the androgynous vision of *Orlando* and *A Room of One's Own*, and to what seems to have been a lesbian affair with Vita Sackville-West (*QB* 2:116–20, 183). For it was that stronger woman, that true King, Mrs. Ramsay, after all, and not that supposed "king in exile" (*TTL*, p. 222), Mr. Ramsay, whom she "wanted" bodily for herself. That, finally, was what was behind her dread of the novel's sentimental theme. She had become a married spinster, as her mother before her had become a married widow, and like Clarissa Dalloway, could join passion with affection only with another woman, and then only fleetingly, clutchingly, as an exultant adolescent crush, and therefore—as sexual liberations go—without much "human gain."[11]

6 Senseless Death

Tuesday, January 17th, 1928

     Yesterday we went to Hardy's funeral. What did I think of? Of Max Beerbohm's letter, just read; or a lecture to the Newnhamites about women's writing. At intervals some emotion broke in. But I doubt the capacity of the human animal for being dignified in ceremony. One catches a bishop's frown and twitch; sees his polished shiny nose; suspects the rapt spectacled young priest, gazing at the cross he carries, of being a humbug; catches Robert Lynd's distracted haggard eye; then thinks of the mediocrity of X.; next here is the coffin, an overgrown one; like a stage coffin, covered with a white satin cloth; bearers elderly gentlemen rather red and stiff, holding to the corners; pigeons flying outside, insufficient artificial light; procession to poets corner; dramatic "In sure and certain hope of immortality" perhaps melodramatic. After dinner at Clive's Lytton protested that the great man's novels are the poorest of poor stuff; and can't read them. Lytton sitting or lying inert, with his eyes shut, or exasperated with them open. Lady Strachey slowly fading, but it may take years. Over all this broods for me some uneasy sense of change and mortality and how partings are deaths and then a sense of my own fame—why should this come over me? and then of its remoteness; and then the pressure of writing two articles and furbishing up the Hardy. And Leonard sitting at home reading. And Max's letter; and a sense of the futility of it all.

                                    A Writer's Diary (p. 122)

For knowledgeable readers the conclusion of the last chapter will seem prematurely grim. Let me amend it to meet their just complaint: to survive as a spinster, married or unmarried, male or female or both, is in modern times (perhaps in any times) a form of human gain. The hero-heroine of *Orlando* (1928) survives the centuries with somewhat forced ebullience; the novelist Bernard defies death with grandiloquent firmness in *The Waves* (1931); the aging Eleanor Pargiter keeps on vaguely venturing in *The Years* (1937); and in *Between the Acts* (1941) the lonely playwright, Miss La Trobe, hears the first words of her next pageant. As these strong survivors attest, creative independence, however isolate, however virginal, is a form of human gain. In moving from Mrs. Dalloway's borrowed and somewhat shaky defiance to Lily Briscoe's more direct ordeal by grief, Virginia Woolf had become her own spinsterly person.

My skepticism in the last chapter is confined to her sexual liberation and its emotional worth. Through Lily's grief in *To the Lighthouse* she was finally able to evoke her long-suppressed and very genuine love for her mother, and so separate it from those confused adolescent yearnings for her which had acquired an erotic dimension since her death. But she had few such yearnings for her father, whose death she would never grieve—nor want to grieve—in fact or fiction; and though she tried hard in *To the Lighthouse* to place him in a romantic light, as in her final gestures toward romantic vowing and lighthouse reciprocity, her fear of and contempt for male passions far exceeded her attraction to them. In effect, Paul Rayley's barbaric fires—or Herbert Duckworth's—still burned brightly; they were, all told, destructive passions, and she could not see them otherwise nor dissociate them wholly from male vowing. But she was free now to gratify her erotic yearnings for her mother with another maternal (if somewhat masculine) woman, her sister-novelist Vita Sackville-West. In a sense she was ready now for romantic marriage with another woman rather than another man. Still, she was in her forties, her erotic inhibitions were newly lifted, her affections were still filial, and her passions were untried. With that precarious equipage she invested her love for Vita with all the romantic ardor and ineptitude of an adolescent crush. It was not, I think, a lesbian affair between equals she then entered—which (putting poor Leonard aside for the moment) one might well want to crow about as "part of the human gain"—but a flighty adolescent love without much passional depth or sexual richness which soon—and not surprisingly—fizzled out. And for me the often forced exuberance and superficial androgyny of *Orlando* speak all too eloquently to its quality.

In *Woman of Letters* Phyllis Rose writes glowingly of the attractions which Vita must have held for Virginia—the artistry of her gardens, the boldness of her sexual escapades, the aristocratic and maternal nature of her charms—as if trying to make her worthy of Virginia's love. But Virginia's worthiness must be questioned too. Was she a fit mate, that is, for the woman who inspired her newfound androgynous vision of 1928 in *Orlando* and *A Room of One's Own?* If her intelligence was superior, as Rose argues, and allowed some room for condescension, did the advantage outweigh her filial affections and untried passions? It seems to me significant, as Rose herself observes, that Vita "was afraid of rousing physical passion in Virginia because of her madness," that she found the very idea of sex with Virginia "incongruous and almost indecent," and that she admitted to bedding with her only twice. Whereas Virginia waxed rhapsodic over that meager experience, boasted about it in letters to Vanessa, chided her for remaining in the "arid garden" of heterosexual love, and dismissed male lovers as dullards: "The scenery of the world takes no lustre from their presence. They add of course immensely to its dignity and safety; but when it comes to a little excitement—!"[1] The excitement was of course immense, the consummation minimal. It was, as Rose observes, the *idea* of having a lesbian affair which excited Virginia. Like Robert Cohn in *The Sun Also Rises*, in his affair with mannish Lady Brett, she preferred the conceptual aura of romance, its literary glow, its aristocratic dazzle, to its deeply felt substance. Which may explain why, as Elaine Showalter insists, her androgynous vision is so transcendentally inhuman, so uninformed by the passional experience of either sex.[2]

The spinsterly gains of her feminist period are nonetheless impressive. As Rose persuasively argues, she achieved political maturity at this time through "her frank concern and affection for women"; her "sympathy for the limitations of their lives" was genuine, and feminism, as "her channel of social concern," brought her closer to their inmost sufferings. In the late 1920s and early 1930s she lectured to female audiences, defended Radclyffe Hall's *The Well of Loneliness*, wrote books, essays, and pamphlets which bravely expressed her newfound sisterly vision. Her feminist anger must also be considered, for in reasoning (as Rose remarks) from her own hurt feelings she was able to detach herself at last from her mother's angelic compliance and her father's patriarchal tyranny. Released in this way from parental bondage, energized by her own peculiar version of lesbian love, she could appraise the male preserve with all the scornful wit and lucid anger at her command.

It seems to me a mistake, however, to confuse her political cogency with emotional and artistic maturity, and to take feminism as "the crux of her emotional [and] intellectual life."[3] For she was curiously divided at this time between militant feminism and impersonal artistry. In her feminist writings she was admirably outspoken, she took courageous stands; yet as an artist she distrusted militancy and struggled to exclude it from her fictions. *The Years* especially suffers from the effort to prevent socially pressing material from spilling over into angry significance. Interestingly, in her first version of the novel, called *The Pargiters, A Novel-Essay*, she tried to channel her divided impulses into alternating sequences of fiction and didactic commentary.

Virginia Woolf had begun this unusual attempt at self-coordination in 1932. She had originally hoped to extend her alternating mix of essays and illustrative episodes from the 1880s to the 1930s; but after sixty thousand words on 1880 alone she had abandoned her ambitious plan, conserved her interspersed arguments for *Three Guineas*, and consigned her fictional episodes to the opening of *The Years*. What stands before us, then, is a spirited hybrid document, an unfinished thesis-novel which in its didactic urgency belies her early scoffing at Bennett, Wells, and Galsworthy, in "Mr. Bennett and Mrs. Brown," for writing novels whose incompleteness moves us "to do something—to join a society, or, more desperately, to write a cheque" (*CE* 1:326). Now Woolf herself attempts to move us by historical persuasion. By taking us into late-Victorian parlors, bedrooms, colleges, and city streets, she tries to demonstrate the devastating effects of male governance on a fictional family much like her own: well-intentioned, "of good social standing," yet hopelessly dispirited.

In keeping with their family name—a "pargeter" is a plasterer or whitewasher, "one who glosses and smooths over"—the Pargiters repress, conceal, evade the pressures and tensions which pervade their restricted lives. As in Katherine Mansfield's famous story, "The Daughters of the Late Colonel," Colonel Pargiter's unfortunate daughters are (in editor Mitchell Leaska's words) "healthy young women sighing in boredom, peeping out of windows at unknown young men, fussing with tea kettles, sexually frustrated and helplessly caged" (TP, p. viii). His more fortunate sons, whose safer access to city streets and privileged access to colleges insures a more informed and active life, are nonetheless reduced to smug self-conquest of forbidden desires and idealized views of desirable mates. And as Woolf points out in her interpretive essays, money and love are the restricting principles by which sons and daughters are alike confined: the money parceled out by their all-powerful (and still extant) father, the love complicated by repressions and taboos, close quarters, the short supply of eligible bachelors, class and financial divisions, and limited mobility. The street-love sequence in which ten-year-old Rose flees from an exhibitionist is used to show why it was "impossible for the Pargiter girls to walk in the West End alone, or to go out after dark unless they had a maid or brother with them" (TP, p. 50); and to show also how glossing and smoothing over sexual realities has made it impossible for the terrified Rose to share her feelings with her pargetting elders.

The late-Victorian ambience, nicely caught in such fictional episodes, is always kept in relevant focus for the sharp analyses that follow. Woolf is especially cogent, for instance, in her many-sided probing of Oxford life: the stuffiness and hypocrisy of the privileged male enclave, the acute social and sexual intelligence of the women forced to cope with it. Her remarks on Kitty Malone's parlor knowledge of body language are alone worth the price of entry (TP, pp. 115–16), and may serve as an instance of how richly the fictional and factual sections support each other. For the immersions in Victorian life are continued in the commentaries with an ease and relevance which make this work unique among feminist documents, and which might well have made it, once completed, the feminist epic of our time.

Indeed, the Malone sections open up alternative possibilities for the treatment of women, following the example of Woolf's favorite male feminist, Joseph Wright, which if pursued might have given this text the balance and contrast of a major thesis novel, comparable in its forceful interpenetrations to similar hybrids like *The Golden Notebook, The Counterfeiters, U.S.A.,* or *Ragtime.* And apparently Kitty Malone, in her loving concern for a spinster history teacher who has "fought her way . . . through obstacles" (*TP,* p. 112), in her exposure to the few radical feminist families at Oxford, and in her yearnings to return to the vital Yorkshire farms from which those families came, was intended to carry that alternative to some appropriate conclusion. But the thrust of this fictive argument is lost in *The Years,* where late in life, Kitty merely returns alone to her titled husband's estate in Scotland, without real point or purpose. The sorry transformations which the novel-portions of *The Pargiters* underwent in *The Years* leave much room for critical speculation. What is clear at this point is that a great enterprise—for reasons still debated—went sadly astray.[4]

Why did Woolf abandon such a promising plan? It was overly ambitious, but no more so than its tedious fictional successor, *The Years,* which attempts to cover the same fifty years of purgatorial pargetting in naturalistic detail, without benefit of commentary. It was more optimistic about solving social problems than she would later come to feel; but if sustained anger is any measure of secret expectations, it fairly matches its analytic successor, *Three Guineas,* where the prospects for social change are far more grim. It was vigorously didactic, in defiance of her early artistic purism; yet its modal mixture exactly suited her need to write alternatively, as she often noted in these years, from different sides of the brain. Indeed, it was the only medium which would have contained her divided impulses while holding reader interest: for it would have forced her to subordinate art to commentary, to select only as much naturalistic illustration as would serve her ongoing arguments, and so avoid the naturalistic quagmire of *The Years*; and it would have forced her also to temper factual coldness with the breathing warmth of fiction, and so avoid the analytic harshness of *Three Guineas.*

Perhaps these last advantages frightened her. As she would later see, her impersonal artistry threatened to absorb and nullify her feminist anger; but more immediately, her feminist anger was disturbing—not to her artistic purism, but to her need to keep in touch as an artist with her deepest personal feelings—her need, that is, to subordinate life to art. If, as I suspect, she was belatedly engaged in the familiar adolescent process of rebellion, then the personal sources of her feminist anger would indeed disturb her. In detaching herself from both parents she might yield to the necessary excesses of rejection and defiance; but she would understandably need to test her insecure reactions within the only medium whose depth, warmth, and wholeness might accommodate their private ranges.

Thus, in the 1880 section of *The Years* she introduces a focal event not present in *The Pargiters*: the interminably protracted passing of the Colonel's wife, Rose Pargiter, a death so nullified by pargetting as to set the family tone for the next fifty years. The episode, as I have argued, is an overcharged amalgam of ill-assorted impressions garnered from Woolf's confused experience of parental deaths in 1895 and 1904. It registers faithfully the dimming of her mother's presence after the *Lighthouse* breakthrough in 1927; but in its stress on interminable dying and false grieving it registers also her belated adolescent determination to dispatch both parents, to project upon them the blame for her own early failure to grieve, and so dispense once and for all with the tiresome burden of her childhood. In her diary recollection of 1934 she had registered the same skepticism about adult pretenses at her mother's death, and had secured her own failure to mourn within the comforting sheath of artistic temperament. Her choice of the naturalistic medium in *The Years* was, in this respect, not unlike her choice of the novel-essay plan in *The Pargiters*: it kept her at a safe artistic distance from this death, it prevented full subjective probing. But it also allowed her to express (through Delia Pargiter) her *present* conscious feelings of rebellion and defiance, of contempt for adult pretenses; and by connecting young Rose Pargiter's night-adventures with her mother's dying, and preserving Colonel Pargiter's anguish, it allowed her to question her protected feelings, to suggest to herself, and perhaps also to her readers, the possible inadequacy of such responses to such a death. Whatever the case, her need to return to the scene of her childhood "crime," to the childhood origins of her angry feelings, is at least a sign of her distrust of her militant feminist outlook, of its capacity to account for the fullness of human experience, or for her intuitive grasp of its fullness. She would be deeply dissatisfied with *The Years*, "that odious rice pudding of a book" (*WD*, p. 280) which required so much forced and ineffectual labor; but she had turned to it from *The Pargiters* in an honest effort to keep faith with her inmost feelings. She would be far more satisfied with *Three Guineas*, to which she had turned from *The Years* so as to conserve her lucid anger from murky pargettings; but in lumping it with *The Years* as "one book" (*WD*, p. 295) she would recognize its comparable incompleteness. In other words, her loyalties were divided, and neither militant fact nor impersonal fiction could contain her troubling self-division.

Had she freed one side of her brain from parental bondage but not the other? That tempting theory might account for the lucidities of *Three Guineas*, if not for the murkiness of *The Years*; but consider for a moment the unacknowledged parental component of her feminist rebellion. In *Three Guineas* she had attacked the patriarchal system with all the resolute independence of her mountain-climbing father. She was like him, moreover, in believing that women should retain their loser's outlook, their outsider's pride, on gaining access to the professions, if only to avoid masculine pugnacity and greed; for the resolute Stephen had also considered himself a loser, and, like other descendents of the Puritan Clapham sect, had prided himself on his outsider's outlook, on what A. O. J. Cockshut has called his "determined, solid, serious unconventionality."[5] More interestingly, she was like her mother in her affection and concern for other women; for not only were her sympathies for their sufferings a selective version of her mother's empathy, they also reflected her own relation with her mother as it fostered social sharing. This will seem paradoxical enough, given her concurrent wish to slay the Angel in the House for schooling her in feminine purity and deference to men; but even that hostility follows from her successful transfer of filial affections to other women. She could afford to slay her mother once she had assumed a feminist version of her mother's role.

But could she altogether afford that mental slaughter? In her reactions to the deaths of friends and literary peers during this period, she would suddenly give way to spasms of self-doubt which, in one way or another, touched upon her feminist sympathies and exposed their maternal sources. These unsettling deaths could easily dispel her confidence in feminist ventures and attachments and in her right or power to pursue them. For, without being innately crucial occasions, they seem to have reawakened her initial sense of worthlessness at her mother's death and so undermined her newfound mode of sharing.

Thus, on September 18, 1927, when she received news of the death of Philip Ritchie, one of Lytton Strachey's many lovers, she was "boiling with the idea" of buying a country house she had visited ten days before with Vita Sackville-West, a serene and sunny place with "endless old rooms." But when she revisited the house with Leonard, after hearing of Philip's death, it seemed "unspeakably dreary; all patched and spoilt; with grained oak and grey paper; a sodden garden and a glaring red cottage at the back." Her reaction to this death had been singular enough: for, after "the usual procession of images," she had felt "for the first time" like "an elderly luggard" who had "no right to go on; as if my life were at the expense of his" (WD, p. 113).

Some six years later, on December 7, 1933, she would react in a similar way on reading "Death of Noted Novelist" on posters in Leicester Square. The novelist in question, Stella Benson, had died in far-off China; but Virginia recalled her now on the terrace at Rodmell when friendship seemed about to burgeon; and again, as with Ritchie, she felt quenched and diminished: "there seems to be some sort of reproach to me in her death, as in K.M.'s [Katherine Mansfield's, in 1923[6]]. I go on; and they cease. Why? Why not my name on the posters? And I have a feeling of the protest each might make; gone with their work unfinished—each so suddenly."

She was herself continuing work on Here and Now, or The Pargiters, her early version of The Years; but the "life" of that work seemed "lessened" by Stella's death, and her own "effusion—what I send out—" seemed "less porous and radiant—as if the thinking stuff were a web that were fertilised only by other people's . . . thinking it too" (*WD*, pp. 213–14).

What Virginia Woolf "sends out"—the fertile sharing of her own creative effusions with others—is not unlike Mrs. Ramsay's delicious fecundity in *To the Lighthouse*, that maternal "fountain and spray of life" by which selfhood is initially nourished, and from which each of us—if we are lucky—develops toward independent being. Virginia's artistic consciousness is fertilized, then, by an emotional sharing like that which she enjoyed in childhood, and is itself a fertilizing bond with others. But as in Donne's famous sermon—"any mans *death* diminishes *me*, because I am involved in *Mankinde*"—it is also diminished by the deaths of others. When Philip Ritchie dies in 1927, the sunny house of life visited with Vita Sackville-West, the inspirer of *Orlando* (then in progress), becomes a dank house of death. When Hardy dies in 1928, Virginia attends his funeral and thinks of her lecture on women and fiction at Newnham College, soon to appear in *A Room of One's Own*; but, observing the event before her, she "doubts the capacity of the human animal for being dignified in ceremony"; and afterward, when Lytton Strachey dismisses Hardy's novels, she wonders why a sense of her own fame comes over her, along with an "uneasy sense of change and mortality" and deathly partings; and she feels "a sense of the futility of it all" (*WD*, p. 122). Again, when the novelist Stella Benson dies in 1933, she feels reproached, depleted, guilty of surviving, and her work on *The Pargiters* loses luster. Her sense of worthlessness at these deaths has something to do, then, with her initial loss of reassuring empathy at her mother's death in 1895. In triumphing over her compliant mother through mental slaughter, in denying her the compassion she now reserved chiefly for professional women and other liberated spirits, she had gained only a shaky foothold on maturity.

In *The Origins of Love and Hate* Ian Suttie holds that the maternal bond in infancy is essentially a socializing bond, an experience of sharing which prepares us for our independent pursuit of shared interests with others in later years.[7] What Virginia

Woolf seems to undergo, in these several deaths, is a reenactment of that initially severed bond, that end to early sharing which left her with such a poorly developed sense of selfhood that she questioned even her own right to live. Behind her sense of futility and her doubts about ceremonial dignity we may posit, then, an apparent halting of her own development as a social and artistic sharer at what seems to be an adolescent stage. That she is open "for the first time" to a definable sense of loss, after writing *To the Lighthouse,* is an important step forward; but the reproachful form it takes suggests again the partial nature of her liberation. She cannot absorb these losses; she still feels implicated in her mother's death, and all her life-directed ventures—the new house, the Newnham lecture, the new book—give way for a time before her continuing sense of guilt. Her predicament is a common one, and may shed some light upon our common difficulties with mourning, our modern skepticism about grieving and its attendant rites and ceremonies. As with Virginia Woolf, it is our failure to assume the old religious burdens, our failure to accept and renew the responsibility for communal sharing, which prevents us from properly mourning our beloved dead. We all know that grief is a devouring emotion which thrives on privacy; we all know that it can diminish self-regard and make "life itself" seem worthless; and yet we cherish privacy too much—or distrust society too much—to act in concert against such damaging effects. We prefer instead those private burdens, those self-reproaches and unresolved relations, which leave us silent and uneasy before enormously important deaths. Having refused the old social and familial functions, having depreciated not merely the social but the human contract, we are unable to find new ceremonies, new modes of sharing grief and absorbing loss, which meet our modern case.

Virginia Woolf's near-solution to this common problem would not be reached until 1939, some twelve years after the completion of *To the Lighthouse,* when, in "A Sketch of the Past," she tried once more to confront the disastrous culmination of her childhood happiness in her mother's death, and the reinforcement of that disaster by ensuing events. Her determination to make her early life available to others was, I think, a form of therapeutic sharing, an inquiry into the causes of her impacted grief, and a delayed exposure of those causes for public contemplation. Granted that she had posterity in mind with almost everything she wrote, and would be safely dead before posterity could respond, her "Sketch" is nonetheless a refreshingly candid appeal for sympathy and understanding, a striking instance of an "effusion" fertilized by the imagined prospect of reassuring empathy.

Simply as a piece of literature, this memoir belongs with her finest work. Her gift for autobiography was in many ways greater than her gift for fiction, perhaps because she was her own best subject. She composed, at any rate, a sensitive and moving recuperation of her early years, remarkable for its honesty and artistry. In it she reassembles and assesses with extraordinary acuteness all her youthful impressions, and, like pieces of an incomplete puzzle, they begin to build and cohere until the break-off-point, November 17, 1940, when she reaches and discusses her hostessing years at 22 Hyde Park Gate.

The sustained self-analysis in these pages seems to me equally impressive. No longer angry with the Angel in the House for superficial reasons—the imposition of purity and of self-effacing deference to men—she unearths the secret causes of her deathbed anger and her lifelong shame, the secret sources of effacement; and, in that long-suppressed context, she recuperates once more her early devotion to her supportive mother, and her early outrage with her tyrannically dependent father, whose superficial toughness had long possessed her, but whose grandfatherly distance from her she now grudgingly acknowledges. Indeed, her return in depth to these considerations, after her heroic feminist rebellion in the late 'twenties and after, seems to me a marked advance in self-awareness, a renewed accommodation of the primacy of love over hate in determining independent growth.

"A Sketch of the Past" is in that sense the heroic highpoint in her lifelong struggle to come to terms with her perplexing parents and—for a short time—with herself. I take it as no accident that, on August 7, 1939, in the midst of her memoirs, she could write in her diary of "how interesting it would be to describe the approach of age, and the gradual coming of death. As people describe love" (*WD*, p. 315); or that on December 22, 1940, a month after her final memoir entry, she could write of her parents:

How beautiful they were, those old people—I mean father and mother—how simple, how clear, how untroubled. I have been dipping into old letters and father's memoirs. He loved her: oh and was so candid and reasonable and transparent—and had such a fastidious delicate mind, educated, and transparent. How serene and gay even, their life reads to me: no mud; no whirlpools. And so human—with the children and the little hum and song of the nursery. But if I read as a contemporary I shall lose my child's vision and so must stop. Nothing turbulent; nothing involved; no introspection. [WD, p. 360]

This may be only an example of the so-called "euphoric" or manic stage preceding her suicide in March; but it seems more plausibly an emotional recuperation and an instance of her own serenity and self-acceptance at this time. Through her "child's vision" she had finally placed her parents with Captain Marryat in that cheerful room with mirrored doors and flowered walls where faith and love transparently abide ("no mud; no whirlpools") and where death becomes a tranquil and fulfilling passage. For the time being at least old ghosts were put to rest. "How one enjoys food now," this notoriously anorectic woman would write on December 29, 1940. "I make up imaginary meals" (WD, p. 361).[8]

But of course the "cure" was incomplete, the meals were never cooked and served. As in 1927, the return of the repressed and the repressive, and her remarkable assessment of it, did not wholly rid her of obsessions. At best, it seems to have given her some respite from impending troubles and perhaps even some strength and health with which to face them. She was able to write her last fine novel, Between the Acts (1941), as she had been able to write (for all its faults) Orlando after To the Lighthouse; and these are her only major fictions which use the past historically and do not elegize her beloved dead, and therefore show some lightening of her burdens.

We may speculate at this point that psychotherapy might have further clarified for her the problem of blocked grief in her childhood and its later consequences, if only by allowing her to sort out for herself the causes of her early anger, or the differences between her own motives for withholding passion in marriage and her mother's, or the origins of her lesbian dependencies, or the sources of her suicidal impulses.[9] But she had done much of this work for herself in her novels and memoirs, and it may be that the primary cause of her approaching suicide lay, finally, outside herself. For many years she and Leonard had treated her madness as an organic nervous disorder (neurasthenia), and had used physical therapy to arrest its onsets.[10] But now age, circumstance, and the world itself conspired against this or any other treatment.

When she felt madness coming on again in March 1941, she was fifty-nine years old, her lesbian affair with Vita Sackville-West was long over, most of her friends and literary peers were dead, her Bloomsbury world and its causes had been eclipsed by the political emphases of the 1930's, and her own feminist protests had been eclipsed by World War II. At this time, moreover, with England under siege, the Woolfs had agreed on suicide should invasion come, their London house had been bombed and their possessions (including the Hogarth Press) had been moved to the country, the pressures and horrors of war had mounted, and in that usual period of depression which followed the completion of her novel that February (*WD*, p. 365), her own defenses were apparently exhausted. "The war is like a desperate illness," she had written as early as May 20, 1940 (*WD*, p. 332). Against the workings of that externally imposed illness her own hard-won health had given way. With some justification, then, we may wish to think of her as a civilian casualty of World War II.[11]

In "A Sketch of the Past," on July 19, 1939, some six weeks before the war began, she had written prophetically of her need of the past in order to live fully in the present, and of the effect of present disruptions upon that need;

> The past only comes back when the present runs so smoothly that it is like the sliding surface of a deep river. Then one sees through the surface to the depths. In those moments I find one of my greatest satisfactions, not that I am thinking of the past; but that it is then that I am living most fully in the present. For the present when backed by the past is a thousand times deeper than the present

when it presses so close that you can feel nothing else, when the film on the camera reaches only the eye. But to feel the present sliding smoothly over the depths of the past, peace is necessary. The present must be smooth, habitual. For this reason—that it destroys the fullness of life—any break—like that of house moving—causes me extreme distress; it breaks; it shallows; it turns the depth into hard thin splinters . . . So I write this . . . partly in order to recover my sense of the present by getting the past to shadow this broken surface. *Let me then, like a child advancing with bare feet into a cold river, descend again into that stream.* [MB, p.98; italics mine]

So she must have walked into the River Ouse that March morning in 1941, to escape those thinning, splintering, hardening present pressures and those obsessive churnings of the past they had reawakened, and to rejoin her beloved dead—Minny and Herbert, Julia and Leslie, Thoby and Stella, and her many early friends and literary peers—in those cold fulfilling depths beyond all splinterings and churnings. She had finally yielded to her lifelong enemy—and by now her oldest and most intimate friend—senseless death.

Notes

1. Converging Views

1. A. O. J. Cockshut, *Truth to Life,* pp. 76–77.

2. As Quentin Bell notes, Woolf assisted in writing a biography of her father in 1904, wrote her first family memoir in 1907 as a "Life of Vanessa," and wrote an obituary on her aunt Caroline Emilia Stephen in 1909 (*QB* 1:90, 122, 143). See also her later obituary or commemorative lives—of her aunt Anny Ritchie, her nephew Julian Bell (*QB* 2:255–59), Lady Strachey (*Books and Portraits*), Janet Case, Joseph Conrad, Thomas Hardy, Roger Fry and others—and her diary responses to the deaths of Jacques Raverat, aunt Anny, Philip Ritchie, Hardy, Lytton Strachey, G. Lowes Dickinson, Stella Benson, Katherine Mansfield, Fry, Case, and James Joyce (*WD*, pp. 8, 72, 113, 122, 179–80, 184, 213–14, 223–24, 285, 363).

3. Helene Deutsch, "Absence of Grief," *Neuroses and Character Types,* pp. 226–36.

4. Jean O. Love, *Virginia Woolf,* pp. 214–16, 291–99.

5. Phyllis Rose, *Woman of Letters,* p. 111. Rose confines her argument to Virginia's immediate difficulties with mourning; the extrapolations as to later difficulties and arrested adolescence are my own.

6. Roger Poole, *The unknown Virginia Woolf,* pp. 30–32.

126

VIRGINIA WOOLF'S QUARREL WITH GRIEVING

7. Elaine Showalter, "Virginia Woolf and the Flight Into Androgyny," *A Literature of Their Own*, p. 268.

8. Mark Spilka, "New Life in the Works: Some Recent Woolf Studies," *Novel: A Forum on Fiction* 12 (Winter 1979): 169–78.

9. Rose, *Woman of Letters*, pp. 70–73.

10. Norman Mailer, *The Prisoner of Sex*, p. 141.

2. The Robber in the Bedroom; or, The Thief of Love

1. A fictional explanation for doubting the sincerity of the nurse's tears is, however, offered in *The Years*. There Delia Pargiter, at her mother's deathbed, observes that one of the nurses is crying, "the one ... who had only come that afternoon" (*TY*, p. 37). She then doubts the sincerity of her father's grief, and later, at her mother's funeral, she has "a convulsive desire to laugh" at her father's stiffness: "Nobody can feel like that, she thought. He's overdoing it. None of us feel anything at all ... we're all pretending" (*TY*, p. 68).

2. Helene Deutsch, *Neuroses and Character Types*, pp. 226–36; Ian Suttie, *The Origins of Love and Hate*.

3. Among recent critics, for instance, Jean O. Love (*Virginia Woolf*, p. 234) and, in effect, Roger Poole (*The unknown Virginia Woolf*, p. 22) support the preoedipal approach while Phyllis Rose (*Woman of Letters*, pp. 111–13) emphasizes the oedipal view by insisting on Virginia's early identification with her father and her readiness for adolescent rebellion. As I indicate in "New Life in the Works," *Novel* 12 (Winter 1977): 173–75, I believe that Rose places that readiness about thirty years too soon. For earlier versions of the oedipal approach, see Nancy Topping Bazin, Mitchell A. Leaska, and Simon Lesser, cited below.

4. In *Woman of Letters* Phyllis Rose takes Virginia's sister Vanessa Bell as the model for Helen Ambrose (p. 57); but as she later acknowledges, Virginia tended to conflate her sister with her mother in her fictions (p. 58) as well as in her personal relations with her (pp. 162, 165).

5. Phyllis Rose also connects Richard Dalloway with George Duckworth as sexual exploiters (pp. 54–55), but misses Duckworth's connection with Rachel's socially exploitive father.

6. For a fuller account of Virginia's literary aunt, see *QB* 1:10–12; 2:42; and *DVW* 1:xx, 247–48.

7. See Virginia's childhood History of the Duckworths, in which she invents a legend for the name's origin: a boy retrieves a duck shot by a king from the middle of a pond and is knighted for it—"Arise Sir

Duckworth, for surely thou art worth many ducks" (*QB* 1:78). See also Mitchell A. Leaska, "Virginia Woolf, the Pargeter: A Reading of *The Years*," *Bulletin of the New York Public Library* 80 (Winter 1977): 181–82, for the connection between "duck" references in her novels, in situations involving death or sex, and the Duckworth side of the family.

8. Deutsch, *Neuroses and Character Types*, pp. 226–29. Deutsch's notion of the "mechanics of narcissistic self-protection" employed by children whose egos aren't "sufficiently developed to bear the strain of the work of mourning" (p. 288) seems especially relevant to Virginia Woolf, as are the situations she posits involving the ego's exhaustion by "some painful occurrence" or its previous engrossment in some narcissistic satisfaction (p. 229).

9. See Nancy Topping Bazin, *Virginia Woolf and the Androgynous Vision*, pp. 70–71. Bazin notes Deutsch's theory of loss but emphasizes oedipal rivalry in *The Years* and elsewhere in accounting for Virginia's failure to grieve. In "Virginia Woolf, the Pargeter" Mitchell Leaska also develops the oedipal attachments in *The Years* of daughters Eleanor, Delia, and Rose to their father, Colonel Pargiter, and connects them all to Virginia's love-hate relation with Leslie Stephen—but not with her grieving problem. Simon Lesser also assumes "competitiveness toward her mother and envy of her father's love of her" in Virginia's childhood, in "Creativity versus Death," *University of Hartford Studies in Literature* 10 (1978): 50.

10. See *QB* 1:82–90, for the protracted death of Leslie Stephen and Vanessa's and Virginia's reactions to it. For Delia as Virginia, see Bazin, *Virginia Woolf and the Androgynous Vision*, p. 70.

11. *QB* 1:13. As Leslie Stephen notes in his *Mausoleum Book*, he had first seen Julia in 1866 at Little Holland House, but had not spoken to her (pp. 30–31); and though he wrote her on several occasions afterwards he did not actually meet her with any social frequency until 1875, the year of his first wife's death—on the eve of which she visited his home. While that situation may have some bearing on Mrs. Flanders's relations with Captain Barfoot in *Jacob's Room*, a more likely candidate for the fictive mistress in *The Years* is the mysterious widow, Mrs. Green, with whom—as Virginia notes with some bitterness—Stephen spent his evenings at some unspecified stage (*WD*, pp. 243–44), most probably after his knighthood in 1902. See also Mitchell Leaska's ingenious notion in "Virginia Woolf, the Pargeter" that the mistress is *The Dictionary of National Biography*, the writing of which kept Stephen from his family (pp. 205, 207).

12. See Leaska, "Virginia Woolf, the Pargeter," p. 181. For the

original text, now in print, see *The Pargiters by Virginia Woolf*, ed. Mitchell A. Leaska, especially pp. 16–17, 38–49, and the essay on street-love and the convention of chastity which follows.

13. *QB* 1:35. Bell fails to place the time of this episode in Virginia's childhood, and Virginia Woolf herself fails to include it in her detailed account of those "moments of being" in childhood, in "A Sketch of the Past," which culminated in her mother's death; but the fact that her fictional version of the episode occurs as a mother dies tends to confirm the connection in her mind between her mother's death and her own early sexual revulsion and defilement, as discussed in her memoir. The connection between rebellion and early exposure to perverse sexuality, which also occurs here, seems to me a cover for that deeper early shame.

14. Usually reliable, Quentin Bell attributes this incident to the twenty-year-old George Duckworth and so misleads many recent critics. His source is a letter from Virginia to Ethyl Smyth, 12 January 1941, in which the "half-brother" responsible for the violation is not named (*QB* 1:44n). But Bell had not read "A Sketch of the Past" in compiling his work, and was thus led by George's known harassments in later years to assume his guilt here. Though George has much to account for, his younger brother Gerald deserves his full measure of blame for initiating Virginia's sexual distress. For more reliable assessments of the episode, see Rose, *Woman of Letters*, pp. 6–8, and Poole, *The unknown Virginia Woolf*, pp. 24–28.

15. Virginia Woolf, *A Haunted House and Other Stories*, pp.18, 19, 93, 99.

16. In *A Literature of Their Own* Elaine Showalter argues plausibly that the onset of menstruation in Virginia's thirteenth year could have produced just such effects (p. 268); but since we are dealing here with the first of a series of major breakdowns, and with a continuing problem of absent grief and recuperative love, such causes seem to me secondary rather than determining. That emphasis aside, there is no real conflict between Showalter's case for the connection in Woolf's mind between "femaleness and death" and the particular fears and fantasies I assess here.

3. Funereal Gloom

1. See Jean Love's account of Stephen's dependent expectations from courtship onwards, in *Virginia Woolf*, pp. 44–47, 78–102.

2. See Love, *Virginia Woolf*, pp. 195, 204–8. Love also holds here (p. 206) that Vanessa's failure to warn Leonard Woolf against moving Virginia to George's household after her 1913 breakdown was either

unwise or inconsistent, given her alleged knowledge and experience of Duckworth's erotic ways in the past. But considering the number of nurses—four—who had to be housed while taking care of Virginia (see Simon Lesser's account here, in "Creativity versus Death," *Hartford Studies in Literature* 10 [1978]: 61), the decision seems to have been an expedient one. There was simply not enough space for the nurses in the Woolf's country home, Asham, and when George—married for nine years—offered his large and well-staffed Sussex home (possibly to make amends for past misbehavior!) the sensible thing was to accept. Vanessa would have had to be steeped in Freudian lore by 1913 to have judged otherwise.

3. For Virginia's preference for older women, see *QB* 1:60–61, 83–84; 2:116–20. See also Jean Love's helpful segment, "How Not to Mourn Julia," *Virginia Woolf*, pp. 296–99, and Phyllis Rose's chapters in *Woman of Letters*, "The Love of Women" and "V. Sackville West and Androgyny."

4. See Poole, *The unknown Virginia Woolf*, p. 32.

5. As quoted in *QB* 1:114–15, from Henry James's letter to Mrs. W. K. Clifford, 17 February 1907 (Harvard University, Houghton Library).

4. Mrs. Dalloway's Absent Grief

1. Virginia Woolf, *Mrs. Dalloway*, Modern Library edition, p. vi.

2. For her increasingly hostile comments on Joyce, see *WD*, pp. 47, 49–50; *DVW* 1:140; and *LVW* 2: 167, 231, 234, 296, 485, 507, 519, 521, 522, 533, 548, 551, 566, 598. Most interestingly, on August 24, 1922, she writes Lytton Strachey: "Never did I read such tosh. As for the first 2 chapters we will let them pass, but the 3rd 4th 5th 6th—merely the scratching of pimples on the body of the bootboy at Claridges" (p. 551). Yet in her diary notation of August 16, 1922, she had been "amused, stimulated, charmed, interested, by the first 2 or 3 chapters—to the end of the cemetery scene" (*WD*, p. 47)—which is the *sixth* chapter and the one she publicly admired in 1919! Only then did she judge what followed the work of "a queasy undergraduate scratching his pimples."

3. In April 1918 Harriet Weaver brought the manuscript of *Ulysses* to the Hogarth Press and asked the Woolfs to consider printing it. Virginia seems to have dipped into the book, then put it away as too indecent. But at least two friends, Desmond MacCarthy and Katherine Mansfield, read portions of the manuscript aloud to her before the Woolfs returned it (nominally for lack of a press large enough to print it, actually to avoid legal prosecution); and by April 1919 she had herself

read chapters appearing in the *Little Review* while preparing her essay on "Modern Fiction." But as her diary shows, she did not read the book straight through until August–September 1922. See *DVW* 1:136; *CE* 2:107; *WD*, pp. 47, 49, 363; and *LVW* 2:242–43.

4. Virginia Woolf reviewed Dorothy Richardson's *The Tunnel* in 1919. Fascinated by the new stripped-down approach to consciousness, she found its application "superficial" but still "vivid" and "convincing" and achieving "a sense of reality far greater than that produced by the ordinary means." Disappointingly, however, it was "surface" reality she offered, an apprehension of present or anticipated surroundings rather than "some new revelation or greater intensity" in probing "hidden depths." All of which suggests that the book's title and method have little or no connection with her own "tunneling process," discovered in 1923, and that Joyce is the more likely source of influence on *Mrs. Dalloway*. See Virginia Woolf, *Contemporary Writers*, pp. 120–22.

5. See Roger Gard, ed. *Henry James: The Critical Heritage*, p. 117.

6. James Naremore, *The World Without a Self*.

7. For Dostoevsky's influence, see her first and shorter version of "Mr. Bennett and Mrs. Brown," *Nation and Athenaeum* 34 (December 1, 1923): 342–43; and see also *WD*, p. 57; *CE* 2:85–86; and "More Dostoevsky," *Books and Portraits,* especially pp. 118–19.

8. See especially Paul Fussell, *The Great War and Modern Memory*.

9. Nancy Topping Bazin, *Virginia Woolf and the Androgynous Vision*, p. 110.

10. In his analytic probings and promiscuous pursuits Peter Walsh may be modeled upon Vanessa's husband, Clive Bell, with whom Virginia enjoyed a long flirtation beginning in 1908, shortly after the birth of the Bells' first child (*QB* 1:132–33, 136, 139, 142, 143–44, 163, 165–66, 168, 171), which flared up again briefly during the composition of *Mrs. Dalloway* (*QB* 2:85–86). Intolerant, brutal, critical of her faults, keenly analytic in his probings of her writings, he spoke eloquently for emotional hedonism and against "sentimental effusions," no doubt in support of his frequent amours after his separation from Vanessa. In a letter of March 1922 Virginia offers what might be a scenario for Walsh's return from India: "I am seeing Clive rather frequently. He comes on Wednesdays; jolly, and rosy, and squab; a man of the world; and enough of my old friend, and enough of my old lover, to make the afternoons hum. Once a week is probably enough! . . . " (*QB* 2:85).

11. On sexual euphemisms in *Mrs. Dalloway's Party*, see John F.

Hulcoop, "McNichol's Mrs. Dalloway: Second Thoughts," *Virginia Woolf Miscellany* 3 (Spring 1975): 3–4, 7; on sexual deletions in *The Years*, see Mitchell A. Leaska, "Virginia Woolf, the Pargeter," *Bulletin of the New York Public Library* 80 (Winter 1977): 172–210.

12. See especially Roger Poole's ill-conceived condemnation of Leonard in *The unknown Virginia Woolf* and Elaine Showalter's much more balanced critique in *A Literature of Their Own*.

13. As recent critics like Poole and Showalter have amply documented, Woolf's indictment here of the coercive and obtuse nature of neurological therapy in the early 1900s and after is well-founded. She had experienced it firsthand, and her outrage against it was surely justified. I am not quarreling with her outraged indictment, but with her use of it to discount suicidal impulses which obviously precede such addled treatment. The absurdities and horrors of "conversion" may promote such impulses, but even empathetic therapy can fail to allay them. Woolf's refusal to confront the real sources of mental illness is the issue here. She sets them forth only to deny them—a point her recent apologists work hard to overlook.

5. Lily Briscoe's Borrowed Grief

1. I. A. Richards, *Practical Criticism*, p. 254.

2. *QB* 1:8. Bell's point here is that Leslie Stephen followed his more manly older brother Fitzjames in this regard, as in many others. See, however, his more natural inclinations as "a nervous, delicate boy, his mother's darling, fond of and over-excited by poetry, too sensitive to be able to endure an unhappy ending to a story," *QB* 1:7. As indicated in the previous chapter, Clive Bell may be another source of Walsh's traits.

3. See Lionel Trilling's remarks on maternal love as the first condition of learning, in "The Immortality Ode," *The Liberal Imagination*, p. 142.

4. See Clarissa's imagined marriage to Peter Walsh, a lifetime of gaiety likened to a five-act play (*MD*, pp. 70–71), as discussed in the previous chapter.

5. Francis Wyndham, "Virginia Woolf, her father's story," *London Times*, Sunday, December 11, 1977, p. 40.

6. A. O. J. Cockshut, *Truth to Life*, pp. 74–76. See also Virginia Woolf's similar views on *The Antiquary*, CE 1:139–43, especially p. 142 on Steenie's death.

7. Indeed, so potent was Duckworth's romantic spirit that his sexual blight on the Stephens' marriage extended even unto the second generation, where Leonard and Virginia Woolf were also described by

their friends as "a Biblical couple, Joseph and Mary" (see Phyllis Rose, *Woman of Letters*, p. 87). For Virginia too was so deeply impressed by his ghostly presence (as well as by his defiling sons) as to withhold herself from passionate love in marriage.

8. See Jean O. Love, *Virginia Woolf*, especially pp. 142, 214–16, 230–34, on the intensity of Virginia's need for her mother's love from infancy onward.

9. I identify Mrs. Ramsay's two companions on p. 299 as Prue and Andrew because Prue has just joined her in death and Andrew's death has been previously on Lily's mind (p. 289) as she ponders old Carmichael's strong reaction to it. But since Andrew died *after* Prue, not before, the grouping on p. 299 is conceivably that of Prue, Mrs. Ramsay, and our unidentified friend noted on p. 270. In which case Mrs. Ramsay may walk on ahead to meet Andrew when he dies.

10. See Leslie Stephen, *The Mausoleum Book*, p. 57, for the actual acceptance scene, and pp. 47–57 for the epistolary vacillations leading up to it. See pp. 30–31 for his 1866 visit to Little Holland House. Stephen places the Venice visit (when Julia first met Duckworth) in 1862, when she was sixteen, and leaves the Lake Lucerne meeting indefinite (pp. 34, 36). In her own memoirs Virginia Woolf collates the Venice visit with her mother's first marriage when she was twenty-one (*MB*, p. 89).

11. For a much more positive view of the benefits of that affair, and of the importance of this phase of Virginia's life, see Rose, *Woman of Letters*, pp. 175–93, 195–224. For my reservations on Rose's views, see the next chapter.

6. Senseless Death

1. Phyllis Rose, *Woman of Letters*, pp. 176–79, 191–92.

2. Elaine Showalter, *A Literature of Their Own*, p. 289. See also pp. 270–75, 295–97.

3. Rose, *Woman of Letters*, pp. xiii, 193.

4. See my review essay, "New Life in the Works," *Novel* 12 (Winter 1977), for further remarks on the failure of *The Years* (pp. 180–85); and note especially my comments on the damaging exclusion of the ironic denouement of the Kitty Malone plot at the proof-stage of *The Years* (p. 182).

5. A. O. J. Cockshut, *Truth to Life*, p. 78.

6. See *DVW* 2:225–28, 317–18, for Virginia Woolf's quite similar—though more confused and complex—reactions to Katherine Mansfield's death in 1923. Along with feelings of rivalry, jealousy, and bitter triumph ("There's no competitor. I'm cock—a lonely cock whose

crowing nothing breaks"), she also feels that her own writing is pointless since "Katherine won't read it," that she has "grown middle aged, & lost some spur to write," and that she will "go on writing, of course; but into emptiness." Her confessed love for Katherine also fits in with the notion of lost maternal empathy I develop here.

7. See especially the first five chapters of Suttie's book, on love, interest, and altruism.

8. See Rose, *Woman of Letters*, pp. 114–15, and Showalter, *A Literature of Their Own*, pp. 268–69, on Virginia's anorectic refusal of food during her mental breakdowns—which Rose interprets as a refusal of maternal nurture, hence a form of rebellion, but which Showalter interprets as a refusal to grow up bodily as a woman. See also Roger Poole, *The unknown Virginia Woolf*, pp. 148–58, on Virginia's justifiable fear of appearing ridiculously fat after medical forced feeding—from which she once gained sixty pounds!

9. Interestingly, Virginia Woolf had begun to read Freud for the first time in 1939 (*WD*, pp. 321–22, 326), a few months after she and Leonard visited him in Hampstead (*QB* 2:209). Ostensibly she read him "to enlarge the circumference; to give my brain a wider scope; to make it objective, to get outside. Thus to defeat the shrinkage of age. Always take on new things. Break the rhythm etc." As her many apologies suggest, she was probably yielding to an urge to take psychoanalysis more seriously as a key to *inner* ills. Her resistance to any kind of invasion of her privacy was, I think, breaking down, and—Quentin Bell to the contrary (*QB* 2:20n)—she might have been persuaded to consult a psychoanalyst at this time. She was conducting her own self-analysis in her memoirs, and over the years she had absorbed a number of popular Freudian concepts, some of which (the relation of childhood to creativity, the impact of the unconscious on conscious life, the therapeutic value of expressing "long and deeply felt emotion") were indigenous to her art; and Leonard, who had read *The Interpretation of Dreams* and had favorably reviewed *The Psychopathology of Everyday Life* in 1914, and who had published Freud's *Collected Papers* in the 1920s, might have worked comfortably with these propensities. But each of them kept such interests curiously separate, to the very end, from the question of her illness; and the nearby doctor and friend, Octavia Wilberforce, to whom they turned under the stressful circumstances of 1941, was again a neurologist. This curious separation of neurological from Freudian views can be seen, incidentally, in Leonard's autobiography for 1911–18, *Beginning Again*, pp. 75–82, 167–68. See also Alix Strachey's belief, in *Recollections of Virginia Woolf*, ed. Joan Russell Noble, pp. 116–17, that Virginia's art and mad-

ness were so intertwined that psychotherapy would have destroyed her art, and that Leonard may have ruled it out on some such grounds—a position at least partly confirmed on p. 80 of *Beginning Again*. One wonders if he would also have ruled out chemical therapy, had it then been available, for her manic-depressive swings.

10. See Showalter, *A Literature of Their Own*, pp. 274–78, and Poole, *The unknown Virginia Woolf*, pp. 121–26 and after, for discussions of the sexist and misogynistic nature of neurological treatment of mentally-ill women patients in the early 1900s. Both critics indict Leonard for conspiring in such treatment with Virginia's neurologists, and so account for Virginia's rage against him during her breakdowns in 1913–15. Neither critic gives Leonard credit for his modified applications of neurological therapy from 1916 to 1941, through most of her productive career. See my *Novel* review, "New Life in the Works," for further remarks on the limitations of Poole's approach to such questions (pp.176–78).

11. This is also Roger Poole's position in the final chapter of *The unknown Virginia Woolf*, though he attributes her suicide wholly to existential despair brought on by the war's disruption and sees no sign of approaching madness. Because he cannot admit that the war might have reactivated lifelong mental problems, or even that she had such continuing and causally related problems from childhood onwards, he is forced to construe her fears of approaching madness in her suicide note to Leonard as a gallant lie. That she killed herself in part to escape from another round of intensive neurological therapy, as Poole also argues, seems to me a more tenable thesis. That much is evident from her note. But her identification of the river's depths with her childhood past is also evident from "A Sketch of the Past" (*MB*, p. 98), and suggests a more fundamental desire to escape from renewed feelings of unworthiness and dependency into the reassuring empathy of oblivion.

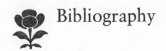

Bibliography

(Works Consulted)

Bazin, Nancy Topping. *Virginia Woolf and the Androgynous Vision.* New Brunswick, N.J.: Rutgers University Press, 1973.

Bell, Quentin. *Virginia Woolf: A Biography.* 2 vols. New York: Harvest, 1972.

Cockshut, A. O. J. *Truth to Life: The Art of Biography in the Nineteenth Century.* New York and London: Harcourt Brace Jovanovich, 1974.

Daiches, David. *Virginia Woolf.* Norfolk, Conn.: New Directions, 1963.

Deutsch, Helene. *Neuroses and Character Types: Clinical Psychoanalytic Studies.* Edited by John D. Sutherland and M. Masud R. Khan. London: Hogarth Press and Institute of Psycho-Analysis, 1965.

Fleishman, Avrom. *Virginia Woolf: A Critical Reading.* Baltimore: Johns Hopkins University Press, 1975.

Fussell, Paul. *The Great War and Modern Memory.* New York: Oxford University Press, 1975.

Gard, Roger, ed. *Henry James: The Critical Heritage.* London: Routledge and Kegan Paul, 1968.

Hawthorn, Jeremy. *Virginia Woolf's Mrs. Dalloway: A Study in Alienation.* London: Sussex University Press, 1975.

Hoffmann, Charles G. "The 'Real' Mrs. Dalloway." *University of Kansas City Review* 22 (Spring 1956): 204–8.

————. "From Short Story to Novel: The Manuscript Revisions of Virginia Woolf's *Mrs. Dalloway*." *Modern Fiction Studies* 14 (Summer 1968): 171–86.

Hulcoop, John F. "McNichol's Mrs. Dalloway: Second Thoughts." *Virginia Woolf Miscellany* 3 (Spring 1975): 3–4, 7.

Kelley, Alice van Buren. *The Novels of Virginia Woolf: Fact and Vision.* Chicago and London: University of Chicago Press, 1973.

Latham, Jacqueline E. M. "The Origins of *Mrs. Dalloway*." *Notes & Queries* 13 (March 1966): 98–99.

————. "The Manuscript Revisions of Virginia Woolf's *Mrs. Dalloway*: A Postscript." *Modern Fiction Studies* 18 (Autumn 1972): 475–76.

Leaska, Mitchell A. "Virginia Woolf, the Pargeter: A Reading of *The Years*." *Bulletin of the New York Public Library* 80 (Winter 1977): 172–210.

Lesser, Simon. "Creativity versus Death." In *A New Anatomy of Melancholy: Patterns of Self-Aggression among Authors.* Edited by

Leonard F. Manheim, M. D. Faber, Harvey I. P. Resnik. *University of Hartford Studies in Literature* 10 (1978): 49–69.

Lewis, A. J. "From 'The Hours' to *Mrs. Dalloway*." *British Museum Quarterly* 28 (Summer 1964): 15–18.

Love, Jean O. *Virginia Woolf: Sources of Madness and Art*. Berkeley: University of California Press, 1977.

Mailer, Norman. *The Prisoner of Sex*. Boston and Toronto: Little Brown, 1971.

Moody, A. D. *Virginia Woolf*. Edinburgh and London: Oliver and Boyd, 1966.

Naremore, James. *The World Without a Self: Virginia Woolf and the Novel*. New Haven and London: Yale University Press, 1973.

Poole, Roger. *The unknown Virginia Woolf*. London and New York: Cambrige University Press, 1978.

Richards, I. A. *Practical Criticism*. New York: Harvest, 1929.

Richter, Harvena. *Virginia Woolf: The Inward Voyage*. Princeton University Press, 1978.

Rose, Phyllis. *Woman of Letters: A Life of Virginia Woolf*. New York: Oxford University Press, 1978.

Sakamoto, Tadanobu. "Virginia Woolf: 'Mrs. Dalloway in Bond Street' and *Mrs. Dalloway*." *Studies in English Literature* (English Literary Society of Japan, English no. 1974): 75–88.

Shelley, Percy Bysshe. *Selected Poems*. Edited by Timothy Webb. London: J. M. Dent, 1977.

Showalter, Elaine. *A Literature of Their Own*. Princeton, N. J.: Princeton University Press, 1977.

Stephen, Leslie. *The Mausoleum Book*. Edited by Alan Bell. Oxford: Clarendon Press, 1977.

Strachey, Alix. In *Recollections of Virginia Woolf*. Edited by Joan Russell Noble. London: Peter Owen, 1972.

Suttie, Ian. *The Origins of Love and Hate*. New York: Agora, 1976.

Trilling, Lionel. *The Liberal Imagination*. New York: Doubleday, 1950.

Vogler, Thomas A., ed. *Twentieth Century Interpretations of "To the Lighthouse."* Englewood Cliffs, N. J.: Prentice-Hall, 1970.

Woolf, Leonard. *Beginning Again: An Autobiography of the Years 1911–1918*. London: Hogarth Press, 1964.

———. *The Journey Not the Arrival Matters: An Autobiography of the Years 1939–1969*. London: Hogarth Press, 1969.

Woolf, Virginia. *Books and Portraits: Some further selections from the Literary and Biographical writings of Virginia Woolf*. Edited by Mary Lyon. London: Hogarth Press, 1977.

———. *Collected Essays*. 2 vols. London: Chatto and Windus, 1966, 1967.

———. *Contemporary Writers*. London: Hogarth Press, 1965.

———. *The Diary of Virginia Woolf*. Edited by Anne Olivier Bell. Vol. 1: 1915–19. Vol. 2: 1920–24. London: Hogarth Press, 1977, 1978.

———. *Freshwater: A Comedy*. Edited by Lucio P. Ruotolo. London: Hogarth Press, 1976.

———. *A Haunted House and Other Stories*. Harmondsworth, Middlesex: Penguin, 1977.

———. *Jacob's Room*. Frogmore, St. Albans, Herts.: Triad/Panther, 1976.

———. *The Letters of Virginia Woolf*. Edited by Nigel Nicholson and Joanne Trautmann. Vol. 1: 1888–1912. Vol. 2: 1912–22. New York and London: Harvest, 1977.

———. *Moments of Being: Unpublished Autobiographical Writings*. Edited by Jeanne Schulkind. New York and London: Harcourt Brace Jovanovich, 1976.

———. "Mr. Bennett and Mrs. Brown." *Nation and Anthenaeum* 34 (Dec. 1, 1923): 342–43.

———. *Mrs. Dalloway*. New York: Harbrace, 1925.

———. *Mrs. Dalloway*. New York: Modern Library, 1928.

———. *Mrs. Dalloway's Party: A Short Story Sequence*. Edited by Stella McNichol. London: Hogarth Press, 1973.

———. *Night and Day*. Harmondsworth, Middlesex: Penguin, 1975.

———. *Orlando*. New York: Penguin, 1946.

———. *The Pargiters: The Novel-Essay Portion of "The Years"*. Edited by Mitchell A. Leaska. New York: The New York Public Library and Readex Books, 1977.

———. *A Room of One's Own*. Harmondsworth, Middlesex: Penguin, 1967.

———. *Three Guineas*. New York: Harbinger, 1966.

———. *To the Lighthouse*. New York: Harbrace, 1927.

———. *The Voyage Out*. Harmondsworth, Middlesex: Penguin, 1975.

———. *The Waves*. New York: Harcourt Brace, 1931.

———. *The Years*. Frogmore, St. Albans, Herts.: Triad/Panther, 1977.

———. *A Writer's Diary*. Edited by Leonard Woolf. London: Hogarth Press, 1975.

Wyndham Francis. "Virginia Woolf, her father's story." Review: Sir Leslie Stephen's *Mausoleum Book*. *London Times*, Sunday, December 11, 1977, p. 40.

Index